LinkedIn

MASTERY

★

For Veterans & Transitioning Service Members

Paul & Mel!

Love you guys!

Thanks for you!

Support!

Adam Braatz

ADAM M. BRAATZ

This book is dedicated to every man and woman—past, present, and future—who answered the call.

Table of Contents

Acknowledgments — **PAGE 7**

Chapter 1 – The Gut Punch — **PAGE 9**

Chapter 2 – Laying the Groundwork — **PAGE 13**

Chapter 3 – Strategic versus Tactical Considerations — **PAGE 22**

Chapter 4 – LinkedIn Profile Essentials — **PAGE 28**

Chapter 5 – The Headline — **PAGE 38**

Chapter 6 – The Rest of Your LinkedIn Profile — **PAGE 44**

Chapter 7 – Building a Powerful LinkedIn Network — **PAGE 57**

Chapter 8 – Stewarding Your New Relationships — **PAGE 64**

Chapter 9 – Creating Content for LinkedIn — **PAGE 75**

Chapter 10 – Important Posting Considerations (Q&A) — **PAGE 80**

Chapter 11 – Be Yourself (Don't Be "That Person") — **PAGE 87**

Chapter 12 – LinkedIn Copywriting Fundamentals — **PAGE 97**

Chapter 13 – Beyond the Text Post — **PAGE 107**

Chapter 14 – Career, Business, & Influence Development — **PAGE 121**

Chapter 15 – Being a Conduit — **PAGE 128**

In Conclusion — **PAGE 134**

Acknowledgments

It took some serious mentorship and support to get my post-service career and life onto the right track. There are so many amazing people I should be thanking that I'm apprehensive to attempt to list them all. I would hate to unintentionally leave someone out. You know who you are. I love you. I'm grateful for you. Thank you.

Most of all, I'm thankful for my amazing wife, Kate, stepdaughters, Chloe and Calla, and son, Phineas, for being the best family a guy could hope for. First off, Kate reviews nearly every word that I publish anywhere, and this book was no exception. She endured the painstaking process of editing this whopper before I sent it off to my professional editor Lori Freeland (who is also awesome and deserving of thanks) and did so joyfully despite not being a veteran, nor an avid LinkedIn user!

I simply couldn't have survived navigating the transition process without my family's love, support, and patience. These outstanding humans saw that I was struggling through my transition before I did. It's crazy how the people we love often know us better than we know ourselves. They helped me to recognize and overcome roadblocks and led me to the realization that my overarching purpose is to help others navigate past those same roadblocks. I want transitioning service members to avoid the same mistakes and hardships I've endured. I want them to be more present, mentally and physically, for their families. I want veterans to realize their potential, achieve holistic post-service success, and find happiness, relevance, and contentment. I want all of you and your families to *thrive*.

I happened upon LinkedIn by accident, really. About nine months before my separation from the military, I made a post on Facebook—"Should I be on LinkedIn?"—that makes me chuckle nearly every time I think about it. I halfheartedly created my LinkedIn profile after my FB pals encouraged me to do so. And then promptly abandoned it to collect dust.

Years later, I was working in fund development for a small nonprofit that had the most elite board of directors with whom I've ever worked. Truly next-level. Among many notable professionals on that board was Wayne Breitbarth, the author of the world's bestselling LinkedIn guidebook *The Power Formula for LinkedIn Success*.

Wayne kindly volunteered his time to sit down with me and show me the ropes. He walked me through profile optimization and taught me how to develop my network in a targeted, strategic fashion. He showed me how valuable a platform LinkedIn could be for professionals of any discipline or industry. I dove in headfirst and never looked back. Nearly every professional opportunity, career advancement, business deal, or fruitful network connection I've been able to establish since that time has been a direct result of LinkedIn, which all can be traced back to Wayne and the time he selflessly dedicated to helping me get started. Thank you, Wayne.

Around the same time that I met Wayne, I was fortunate to connect with Andy Locke. Andy is a prolific major gifts fundraiser and the most talented relationship builder I've ever met. Even though Andy was technically mentoring me about fundraising techniques at the time, we rarely spoke about how to actually ask people for money. His approach was based almost entirely upon serving others, getting to know them personally, and connecting them with other professionals who could help them solve their problems. The "ask" was almost a secondary, or heck, even tertiary consideration. To the untrained eye, his approach may sound counterintuitive. *A fundraiser not focused first and foremost on raising funds? Surely you jest!*

Andy's unparalleled success speaks for itself. He understands what inspires and motivates his connections and fosters such impressive levels of genuine trust that his pitches are never awkward or damaging to his relationships. In fact, I wouldn't even call them pitches—just casual conversations between good friends. No pressure, no conning, no manipulation, no negativity. Not only does he get the job done at a high level, but I'm guessing both he and his donors sleep soundly.

Andy's mentorship played an integral role in my understanding of the immense power of professional network development, the value inherent in being known as a "guy who knows a guy/gal," and the joy of connecting others. He wasn't excessively active on LinkedIn, nor did he need to be. A vast majority of his clientele was old-school, and he thrived in their ecosystem. Thanks for everything, Andy.

Approaching network development with that old-school, face-to-face mentality is the name of the game, even on a digital platform. In-person networking and online networking are two sides of the same coin. Yin and yang. When you develop both angles with a unified, service-oriented approach, there is no end to what you can accomplish. To quote legendary rapper Del the Funky Homosapien (out of context, of course), it's "the perfect blend of technology and magic."

Finally, my most sincere gratitude to LinkedIn and their whole crew, especially their military affairs team. This team has made something truly special and continually proves their commitment to the user experience as well as the veteran community. I must add that this guide is in no way officially connected with nor endorsed by LinkedIn, Microsoft, or any of their employees or affiliates. There is a paragraph or two of legal mumbo jumbo around here somewhere.

All of that red tape aside, thanks LinkedIn. You're great.

CHAPTER 1

The Gut Punch

I was honored to serve in the United States Air Force on active duty from 2008 until the end of 2015. During my first enlistment, I worked under the greater wing of Air Force Public Affairs as a bandsman. It was with this team that I found myself traveling throughout the Middle East on a mission to support deployed troops and forge relationships with foreign dignitaries and residents throughout Iraq, Oman, Qatar, United Arab Emirates, Kuwait, and Kyrgyzstan. An eye-opening experience to say the least. Each country seemed like a different planet. During this mission, I witnessed the true impact of our collaborative global efforts for the first time and experienced great pride to be part of this movement.

It was a complete mindset reversal. Prior to this deployment, I'd been knee-deep in fantastical plans to complete my four-year commitment to the Department of Defense and then bail. At that time, my brilliant idea was to move out to Los Angeles, attend graduate school, and fulfill my destiny as a studio musician. It seems so silly in hindsight, but back then it was the only future I could imagine. Nothing against professional or studio musicians at all—it was only a nonsensical ambition for me because it was not my true calling. Not even close.

After returning stateside, I felt overwhelmed by a combination of loyalty to the Air Force and eagerness to prove myself. Beyond ready for the next chapter, I reenlisted, promptly applied to be an instructor at enlisted basic training at Lackland Air Force Base in Texas, and was accepted. It was a drastic shift, and I distinctly remember my fellow bandsmen thinking I'd lost my mind. Turns out it was the very challenge I'd been looking for. Which just goes to show that sometimes you need to go with your gut. Even when everyone around you is threatening to have you committed.

Serving in the Military Training Instructor (MTI) Corps was an utterly transformative professional experience. Coming from a career field in the Air Force Bands, which was significantly more relaxed, I had some severe growing pains to overcome but quickly found my footing and excelled. The training and certification process was grueling and demanding but absolutely top-notch across the board. I was a different person by the end of it. I could write another book with the stories I have from that period in my life.

Being a basic training instructor is about as entertaining as you can imagine, though the whole ecosystem has been sensationalized in popular culture. Yes, I raised my voice. Yes, I marched people around. Yes, I made trainees do push-ups. Did any of us instructors channel R. Lee Emery in Full Metal Jacket? Heck no. We were professionals. Our training environment was strictly monitored and regulated. Every single move we made and every single thing we said was required to be connected to a verified training objective. If we stepped out of line by overtraining, ostracizing, or hazing, we risked severe punishment. Though we needed different tools in our toolbox than our predecessors, the elite professionals I served alongside in the MTI Corps still managed to maintain the persistent level of excellence required for optimal learning in a training environment.

Don't get me wrong—yelling was definitely a staple of being an instructor. And a great stress reliever. But it wasn't my favorite part. During this enlistment, under the umbrella of Air Education and Training Command, I discovered a love for education and mentorship. And that love strongly influenced my post-military career trajectory. I discovered that my passion was in helping others overcome obstacles, grow, and realize their true potential. This enduring purpose manifested in a truly diverse, interdisciplinary career that will likely continue to evolve. I often say that I've lived a bit of a "Forrest Gump life" due to the seemingly random, nonlinear nature of my professional path. If you don't get the reference, well, put this book down and go watch Forrest Gump now. You can thank me later. And you will.

I'm grateful for each and every experience and the incredible connections I was fortunate to make along the way. It may sound cliché—and I won't apologize for it—but only fellow veterans can truly appreciate the depth and quality of the relationships developed during service. It wasn't easy to walk away from the people, the institutions, and the mission, but I had done my part to the best of my ability and elected to move on.

Everyone has individual motivations for separating or retiring from the military. Some do so voluntarily. Others are forced out due to circumstances beyond their control, like injury or force reductions. A few folks drive off base for the last time with their middle fingers held high—literally or figuratively—while more than one or two will weep uncontrollably at their retirement ceremonies, unable to fathom life without military service. I've observed all of the above.

I decided to separate from the military for many reasons but without an ounce of contempt for the US Air Force. At the top of my list was a desire to be more in control of my time, location, and overall destiny. I was tired of being geographically separated from my family. I felt I was ready to rejoin the rest of humanity and try my hand at private sector life.

While still on active duty, I spent a great deal of time daydreaming about what I "wanted to be when I grew up" and eventually decided on the nonprofit world. I had no personal experience in that world whatsoever—aside from random volunteer work during service—but it sounded perfect to me in theory. I desired to capture that euphoric feeling of impact and purpose that I had experienced during my deployment and subsequent time in the MTI Corps. I wanted to sleep soundly every night knowing I'd dedicated myself to helping and mentoring others. Nonprofit work seemed like a logical fit.

There is also the possibility that I overflowed with an abundance of naive altruism.

At any rate, I obtained a Master's in Nonprofit Development and Program Management, attended my congressionally mandated transition assistance program, and waited for the civilian job offers to roll in. In hindsight, getting a niche master's degree in a specialized field in which I had zero real-world experience may not have been the wisest choice. At the time, I thought that my master's coupled with nearly a decade of work experience and top-notch productivity would be more than enough to land me an upper-level executive position in the nonprofit industry.

I quickly learned that wasn't the case. Experience matters. Relevant experience matters more. And formal education does not close the gap between the two. In most cases, the degree merely empowers you to close that gap more quickly. To make matters worse, civilian employers often do not consider military service to be work experience at all.

Sometimes I look back and wonder how on earth I could've been so woefully unprepared for the "real world." In my defense, I simply didn't know what I didn't know. To add another layer of complication, none of the folks tasked with preparing me for my transition had experience on the "other side." They didn't know what they didn't know either. It was the blind leading the blind. Or like a fresh second lieutenant trying to lead a gaggle of fellow butter bars out of a forest.

My transition story is a typical one in many ways. I spent a few months unemployed and then endured years of underemployment. I learned very quickly that the nonprofit world is strange, unpredictable, and unforgiving. Like many specialized industries, everyone must pay their dues no matter where they come from and for good reason. Now I understand that I wouldn't have had success as a senior civilian leader straight out of the military. I wasn't ready. At the time, however, I took great offense to the mere suggestion that I couldn't dive right into that role.

The blow to my ego was almost too much to bear. Hadn't I already paid my dues? I'd just come from the elite Military Training Instructor Corps. Been a respected subject-matter expert. Mentored hundreds of trainees. So why was I shoved down to the bottom of the nonprofit ladder? These childish, self-centered thoughts clouded the bigger picture. While potential employers failed to recognize the experience I did bring to the table — due to a combination of subconscious prejudice on their part and an abysmal failure to convey it adequately on my part — I also grossly overestimated the relevance of my experience.

Many veterans fight the same battle with their egos as they first transition into the civilian workforce, which is yet another ancillary consequence of poor preparation. The whole situation is more than infuriating, it's potentially life-threatening. We're talking about lives and livelihoods here. More on that later.

As veterans often do, I bounced from job to job in an effort to procure a "good fit." I clawed my way up. I used salary increases in new positions to justify laughably short tenures. I contemplated a wide variety of potential next steps—going back to school, signing up for my local police academy, or trying my hand at retail management to name a few. I wasted countless hours applying for completely random jobs that would not have been good for me or the businesses to which I was applying.

I'm sure you noticed the title of this book when you picked it up. So, what does all of this have to do with LinkedIn? Exactly everything.

While it is possible to land your dream job the old-fashioned way, the odds are against you. Even when the leverage needle is pointed in favor of the career seeker—as it is at the time of writing this book in the shadow of the "great resignation"—there is still a nearly endless supply of candidates being scrutinized by an equally bountiful supply of functional recruiters. I don't envy those on either end of the spectrum right now.

My post-service career truly began to take shape when I started to devote more time to developing my professional network. It turns out that the adage "it's all about who you know" is 100% accurate. So is "your network is your net worth." They're both true in almost every single professional endeavor you'll undertake. The absolute best way to make the sale, land your dream job, score that big promotion, successfully pitch a project, or launch a scalable business is by leveraging a powerful, organically developed network. And what is the single most effective tool to do that? As of today, LinkedIn.

The information, techniques, and practices in this book—with LinkedIn at the center—are the foundation of a fulfilling post-service career and life. I wish I would've known all of this prior to my transition, which is why I enthusiastically evangelize about it today. In fact, "I wish I would've known . . ." is what inspired me to write this book in the first place.

I'm honored that you've picked it up. Now, let's get to work.

CHAPTER 2

Laying the Groundwork

I have a confession to make.

When I'm excited about diving into a book, *especially* a technical manual of any kind, I often skip the preface, acknowledgments, foreword, about the author, or any introductory material that may get in the way of my entertainment and education. I know many out there who do the same. Now that I've written a book myself, I have a greater understanding and appreciation for the value of laying some groundwork like this.

You're probably excited to get started. I don't blame you, but this stuff is important. That's why I don't have a foreword section in this book at all—to keep you on your toes. The ole bait and switch for impatient people like yours truly. Now that you know what's up, still don't even think about skipping this chapter. It's worth the time, I promise.

Throughout this book, you'll find boxes with links to external resources, supplemental considerations, or essential privacy and security information. I implemented these asides for emphasis and to break up the monotony. Who wants to read an endless stream of bulk text? Not me. Besides, they look cool. And I worked really hard on them.

 HEADS UP!

These boxes provide information regarding your security, safety, or privacy. There are scammers and trolls around every corner — it's best to always have your guard up.

A few — but definitely not all — the external links in the "Check It Out!" boxes are affiliated or eventually lead to an affiliated link of some kind. This means that they link to a product or service that could have a fee attached. In some cases, if you decide to make a purchase using one of my affiliate links, I may get a small commission. This doesn't add any cost on your end. To the contrary, actually. As an affiliate, I have the opportunity to provide the best possible deals on these products or services to my network. But please always do your own research when it comes to any product, service, or digital subscription.

I usually encourage people to avoid shelling out their hard-earned cash and will suggest ways to work around having to do so whenever possible. It's important for me to express that I would never recommend anything to you that I didn't entirely believe in myself. For example, later in the book, I suggest signing up with Canva for simple digital design needs. Canva is a completely free service that also has paid premium features that most people don't need for basic use. I use it almost every single day and swear by it.

HYBRID CONSIDERATIONS

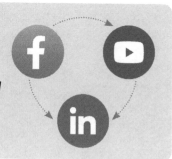

These boxes provide suggestions on how to expand your overall digital footprint and brand by repurposing your content from LinkedIn on other platforms.

THE STATE OF VETERAN EMPLOYMENT IN THE UNITED STATES

From time to time, I reflect upon my first post-service job. I was just so thankful to have a gig. It was an answer to our family's prayers. There's something supremely unsettling about the uncertainty of a career transition when coming out of an institution like the United States military. In that first job, I'd been hired as an entry-tier executive for a long-standing national nonprofit organization dedicated to youth mentorship and education, which I believed to be aligned with my goals and values. Despite holding a shiny new graduate degree and over a decade of work experience, I was salaried at $36,000 with negligible benefits. It was something, and of course, something is better than nothing, right?

Maybe not. I had no idea that salaries, especially lower salaries, are often used to exploit workers. Employees are drawn in by the perception of security that accompanies a salaried position, then are asked to work long and unconventional hours. This is, unfortunately, very common in the nonprofit world. Doing the math to calculate what an hour of my effort was worth based on my salary and the time I was putting in was a sobering experience.

I hadn't yet heard the term "underemployed." Underemployment is an often-overlooked situation in which an employee is compensated far below their value or capabilities. It can be a troublesome circumstance, dragging the employee down physically and mentally so they don't have the energy or confidence to find more appropriate work. In that job, I was tragically — borderline laughably — underemployed. The charter that hired me wasn't actively trying to take advantage of me. They had their compensation tiers firmly established through their national umbrella organization, and my immediate leadership didn't have much wiggle room. Besides, nonprofits typically run fairly close to the margins as it is. There is plenty of money to be made in the nonprofit world, of course, but usually not for entry-level folks. They truly were doing the best they could do for me, even if the salary seemed predatory at best.

The fact remained that I was essentially getting paid the same as an employee fresh out of undergrad. With a growing family at home, this stretched us to the point of discomfort. For the hours I was working — far beyond the customary forty hours a week that qualify an employee as full-time — I would've been better off, in the short term at least, in an hourly position as a retail assistant manager or gas station attendant. Think about that for a minute. For real.

Unemployment and underemployment are serious issues for the veteran community. Surprisingly, data on unemployment has consistently shown veterans unemployed at a lower rate than the rest of the civilian world, but these figures don't tell the whole story and leave the concept of underemployment out entirely. As I mentioned earlier, unemployment and underemployment for veterans can be potentially life-threatening situations. Transitioning from an all-encompassing institution like the United States military is challenging enough. But adding the financial and emotional burden of unemployment or underemployment to the mix? Ouch.

CHECK IT OUT!

For some mind-blowing data and statistics on the state of veteran life and employment today, check out Pew Research Center's "The American Veteran Experience and the Post 9/11 Generation":

 https://pewrsr.ch/32uqNJs

Underemployment may very well be more dangerous for veterans than unemployment. Underemployed professionals often find it challenging to muster the energy and confidence to network or go through exhausting application and employment processes while working long, laborious hours. I've seen lengthy periods of underemployment whittle down even some of the most elite military professionals.

Simply put, underemployment is a trap that can prevent people from realizing their true professional potential, and it happens in the veteran community at catastrophic levels. Why? Not from a lack of work experience or education. Studies show that veterans hold degrees, advanced degrees, and certificates at a higher rate than the general public.

There are several factors, in my opinion, that contribute to the underemployment epidemic in the veteran community. Both employers and career-seekers have a lack of understanding of the military professional experience. As I mentioned above, many employers refuse to consider military experience as work experience at all. The average civilian has no grasp on the diverse and in-depth training that the average service member receives during their tenure in the military. On the flip side, veterans often struggle with translating their skills in a way that is relevant to a civilian hiring manager. Or like in my case, they may overestimate how attractive their skills and experiences would be. This subject alone is the topic of entire books.

CHECK IT OUT!

LinkedIn truly puts their money where their mouth is when it comes to supporting the veteran community and uses data to drive their decisions in the space.

From LinkedIn: "The Veteran Opportunity Report, powered by LinkedIn data and insights, explores the current state of veteran employment and how challenging it can be for veterans to face the realities of not doing work that makes use of their skills and abilities."

Read the LinkedIn Veteran Opportunity Report here:
https://socialimpact.linkedin.com/programs/veterans/veteran-opportunity-report

I've been accused of exaggeration in the past when referring to the severity of unemployment and underemployment situations for veterans. I can assure you, I'm not exaggerating. Many veterans struggle with separating their sense of value from their employment. It makes sense if you think about it. Serving in the military is more than just a job. You're on-call and held to certain standards twenty-four hours a day, seven days a week. You live, work, shop for groceries, and go to the doctor on base. A military service member's identity is inherently tied to their employment or, at the very least, more closely tied than the average civilian's. It's understandable that many veterans fixate on their civilian jobs after hours, work later than required, and take dissatisfying periods at work harder than their civilian counterparts. I know I did. Heck, I still do.

Why does this matter? Transition is a serious upheaval that affects much more than just employment. In fact, the idea that transition is over once a vet secures post-service employment can be downright life-threatening. Transition is an ongoing process. It doesn't end when employment is secured. This endeavor is more significant, nuanced, and far-reaching than the typical career transition — which is hard enough on its own. Service members are leaving more than just a job. Military service is a way of life that impacts all pillars of wellness. Any tools we can put in our toolbox to cope with and overcome the stressors of transition are invaluable.

WHY MASTERY?

It's important to take a moment to talk about the title of this book as well as the definition of mastery as I see it. Some mistakenly interpret mastery as 100% knowledge or capacity on a given subject. If that were true, no person would be able to attain true mastery of anything ever. After all, as Einstein famously said, "The more I learn, the more I realize how much I don't know."

Most accurately, mastery can be defined as the ongoing pursuit for effortless competence. The mastery of LinkedIn is no different. It's a continual quest for comfort, growth, leverage, and opportunity within the confines of the platform. But you'll never know everything there is to know about this platform. And even if you could achieve such a feat, LinkedIn changes so frequently that the accomplishment would be fleeting. I consider myself exceptionally competent at LinkedIn and still find that I'll learn something new or tweak my approach daily.

Accordingly, I won't ask for nor will I promise perfection. Perfection is irrelevant. Progress is what matters. You don't need to come anywhere near "perfection" to leverage LinkedIn for some serious prosperity and opportunity.

Mastery is an interdisciplinary concept. No one can truly "master" anything by focusing exclusively on that one thing. In this respect, singular focus can be a hindrance. For example, an aspiring all-star baseball player can only achieve mastery of the sport by also having a fundamental understanding of physiology and nutrition. Musicians must understand marketing and brand management. Financial managers must learn how to play golf. The list goes on.

Complementary skills are a fundamental key to mastery of any subject. If you're looking for only a LinkedIn technical manual, you're in the wrong place. A technical manual would enable your base proficiency, not mastery. I spend a fair chunk of this book discussing topics on the periphery. They're all relevant to your journey toward LinkedIn mastery, and in turn, your post-service success.

This is where your mindset has its most profound impact. To achieve an impactful level of mastery at LinkedIn and unlock its full potential, you must have a wide variety of networking, branding, marketing, and writing tools at your disposal. By reaching an adequate level of comfort in these types of complementary skills and consistently using them, anyone can become an elite force with which to be reckoned. Throughout this book, I'll discuss these skills and the many valuable lessons I've gleaned from wise mentors along my personal path toward LinkedIn mastery.

These hybrid considerations, as I call them, are important for several reasons. First, your newfound skills will be transferable to a variety of settings. Second, having a developed presence on a variety of platforms leads to a snowballing effect—the platforms cross-pollinate and bolster one another. The content you use to reach your target audience can be reused and repurposed in many ways across many platforms. Your connections on LinkedIn will be more likely to follow and engage with you elsewhere and vice versa. It may seem like a foreign concept, but it's absolutely true that a strong LinkedIn presence can help you grow your face-to-face network, that a developed Instagram platform can help you on TikTok, and so on. All your networking, branding, and influence boats rise together.

Finally, consider what would happen if LinkedIn were to disappear. What if you were to be permanently banned from the platform for one reason or another? I've seen more than one prominent influencer banned by mistake or misunderstanding, only to be left in complete social media darkness until everything got sorted out. In one case, it took several months, which had a catastrophic effect for that person's brand. What if the machines revolt against us, our entire global digital network fails, and we're forced to network exclusively the old-fashioned way—while dodging murderous robots? There's a very slim chance that any of those circumstances will come to pass, but best risk management practices suggest not tossing all your eggs into a single basket. You could call this network diversification.

WHY LINKEDIN?

Not long after Microsoft purchased LinkedIn in 2016—for the very hefty sum of $26.2 billion—they dove into a truly ambitious and revolutionary project. Enter the LinkedIn Economic Graph. The Economic Graph is a digital map of the world's economy, representing all three billion humans in the global workforce. From LinkedIn CEO Jeff Weiner:

> **"**
>
> *We are going to have a profile for every member of the global workforce. We're going to have a profile for every company in the world. We are going to have a digital representation of every job and every skill required to obtain those jobs. We are going to have a digital presence for every higher educational organization and university. We want to make it easy for every individual, every company, and every university to share their professionally relevant knowledge to the extent they are interested. In doing so, the hope is that we can lift and transform the global economy. It's not enough to just standardize the data around the skills required to obtain a role. It's important that we are training today's workforce for the jobs that are and will be, not the jobs that once were.*
>
> **"**

LinkedIn is making strides toward that vision. As of this writing, they have over 800 million users, 58 million companies, 120,000 schools, and 38,000 skills represented on their platform. Truly incredible numbers.

It's easy to tell that I'm fairly bullish on LinkedIn. It's not just another social network. It isn't Facebook or Instagram or TikTok or Bumble. LinkedIn is the world's largest professional database—that just happens to have a social aspect attached to it. This database is powerful and far-reaching with more than 175 million users in the United States alone. A LinkedIn profile has become a baseline expectation for modern professionals. At first glance to the novice, the social aspect may have a similar vibe to Facebook, but the ecosystem is entirely different. And we must approach it differently.

There are a handful of quality publications about LinkedIn out there, so why on earth would I devote my time to write another one specifically for veterans? In addition to the sobering post-service employment situation facing the veteran community, I've witnessed trends in the digital landscape that are exclusive to veterans and military families, especially the newly transitioned, that need to be addressed.

Though aspiring LinkedIn rockstars who aren't military members, spouses, veterans, caretakers, surviving dependents, or veteran advocates—in other words, people in the military and veteran bubble—would undoubtedly find value in about 92% of my advice, I didn't write this for them. Simply put, veterans not only need the focused attention, they deserve it. If you're outside the bubble, you're still very welcome to read on. I hope you enjoy the book, and I'm confident you'll get a lot out of it.

Through LinkedIn, I've seen countless veterans overcome unemployment and underemployment, develop their careers, earn promotions, grow influential brands, and cultivate powerhouse networks. Whether you're interested in working for a private company, landing a government job, or braving entrepreneurship, you absolutely must have an active presence on LinkedIn, cultivate your brand, and steward your relationships.

Many corporate employees long for entrepreneurship. Many nonprofit employees wish to move into a more secure employment situation. Chances are, you will transition again at some point in your career, and your online brand will be the common thread that connects and enables you to succeed. This time around, the transition shouldn't be as complicated or stressful as when you left the military. But regardless, your prospects will depend upon the power of your brand and network—in person and online.

I'm often told by my clients that LinkedIn "is for old people" or that they avoid creating content because they're not in the market to "become an influencer." I try not to roll my eyes. At least on the outside. First, demographic data shows that LinkedIn users are more diverse and versatile than ever before. Second, the user base is steadily becoming younger as time goes on.

Don't worry about becoming an influencer. It isn't easy, nor does it happen by accident. Imagine someone who's never worked out saying that they don't wish to start lifting weights because they don't want to "get too muscular," as if they'll wake up after a few sessions and be radically transformed into Mr. Olympia 2.0 overnight. These types of endeavors take vigilant, consistent work over long periods of time. Sharing original content a few times a week isn't going to magically make you Internet famous. Even if you had a single post go massively viral, keeping your new audience takes hard work. If you're feeling self-conscious about sharing content and are worried others might see you as a wannabe influencer, just stop it. Most of the people who hate on content creators and use the term "influencer" in a negative way aren't worthy of your concern anyway.

Every networking platform has both good and bad aspects. And I'm committed to giving you the full picture when it comes to LinkedIn. Like every other online platform, it has scammers, takers, and fakers. There are self-indulgent engagement grabs, fake bologna, and spamming. There are con artists and trolls. Don't let that deter you. These factors are on every platform—digital or analog, online or in person—and navigating around them is just part of life. Throughout this book, I share some simple tactics you can use to guard yourself against the noise so you can get down to business.

There are plenty of people out there who passionately hate LinkedIn. In my experience, nearly every person who claims "LinkedIn doesn't work" is not using it correctly. It really is that simple. Perhaps you're one of those people, and you're reading this with skepticism. I get it. Despite its few flaws, LinkedIn really is an incredible platform. Hang in there. You won't regret it.

 HEADS UP!

If you are running into any issues or bugs, have a great idea for a new feature, or want to grab LinkedIn's attention in any way, try tagging LinkedIn in a comment or post by typing @, then selecting LinkedIn from the dropdown menu.

This will automatically generate a ticket for LinkedIn's staff to take a look at.

CHAPTER 3

Strategic versus Tactical Considerations

In my experience, there are few things more infuriating than receiving strategic-level advice when you're looking for tactical guidance or vice versa. Given the rapidly evolving nature of web platforms, most authors avoid giving tactical advice in traditional printed publication. I can sympathize with why, but it still drives me nuts. I remember how disappointed I was after purchasing a "comprehensive" guide to YouTube in hopes of receiving step-by-step instructions, only to discover that the entire thing was strategic fluff. The book would've been perfect if I'd needed a big-picture overview, but I didn't.

Alternatively, beginners often need to understand big-picture concepts and can get bogged down and overwhelmed by intricate details. Both strategic and tactical approaches have their time, place, and value. To give you the most comprehensive picture, this book will provide guidance from both perspectives—the view from thirty-thousand feet as well as the view from boots-on-the-ground.

With this approach, do I run the risk of certain tactical aspects becoming obsolete or outdated? Perhaps. It's nearly impossible to make anything about the Internet future-proof, but you deserve real-deal, tactical-level advice without having to comb through a mountain of individual blogs, articles, or YouTube videos to find it.

I will start by giving you the full rundown on optimizing your profile, settings, and notifications. After you've polished your LinkedIn presence, we'll work on developing a large, diverse, and powerful professional network online. Next, we'll dive into the best practices for content creation with examples on how to build a massive platform of influence. Finally, we'll bring it all together with tips on leveraging all the above for your career and business endeavors.

ASSUMPTIONS

For the purposes of this book, I'll assume you know how to use a computer and a mobile device as well as register an account on an online platform or social network. You don't need expert technological aptitude or IT certifications to make this happen, but if you have a hard time registering an email to get a profile started, you may need some "tech" training before diving into this book.

If you do struggle with the tech aspect or don't have the resources (computer, Internet connection, etc.) to make this happen, your local library or community center will be able to help you. Additionally, there are many nonprofit organizations throughout the country which exist to help veterans get connected.

That said, LinkedIn is fairly intuitive, and I believe most veterans will be able to figure it out. After all, the base level of tech competence for vets is generally higher than for the average citizen.

Lingo – Common Terms to Know

- ⊛ **Company Page** – a separate profile page for a company, business, or brand.

- ⊛ **Connection** – your degree of connection in relation to other users is rated as 1st, 2nd, or 3rd+ and is visible as you interact with other users or view their profiles.

- ⊛ **1st-Level Connection** – similar to "friending" someone on Facebook, connecting is a mutual agreement of interaction. 1st-degree connections will be able to view your full profile and your connections, and your content will appear in their newsfeed. Each user is allowed a maximum of 30,000 1st-degree connections.

- ⊛ **2nd-Level Connection** – folks who are connected to your 1st-degree connections. Your mutual connections. Your "friend of a friend" people.

- ⊛ **3rd+ Level Connection** – think "three degrees of Kevin Bacon" here. This is the furthest you can get from Kevin Bacon if Kevin Bacon is a LinkedIn user.

- ⊛ **Creator Mode** – turning on "Creator Mode" changes the layout of your profile page and is intended for users focused mainly on content creation.

- ⊛ **Direct Message** – also referred to as a "DM." This is the private chat feature and a powerful tool for your network development and cultivation. Some call this a "private message" or "PM."

⊛ **Feed** – your "newsfeed" and the large central column of your LinkedIn main page. This is where content from your connections, influencers, and the company pages you follow shows up. LinkedIn will also feed you content it believes will be relevant or intriguing to you along with a manageable amount of promotional material. Your feed can be a source of information, connection, news, and uplifting content. It can also be a source of negativity and nonsense. Curating your newsfeed is exceptionally important to ensure that the content stays valuable and relevant and doesn't take an undue toll on your positivity and mental health.

⊛ **Following** – when you follow a member, company, or content creator, that content becomes eligible to end up in your feed. It is possible to follow someone without connecting with them. This is the most likely scenario when you wish to follow companies or famous people.

⊛ **Group** – a voluntary collective of LinkedIn users united by a common interest, ideal, or demographic.

⊛ **Influencer** – a person who has the ability to inspire thought and behavior in large groups of followers.

⊛ **InMail** – direct messages with some added oomph. These messages have a 1900-character limit with the option of an added 200-character subject line, and you don't need to be directly connected with the recipient to send one. InMails are believed to have a higher open and conversion rate, but the number you can use freely is limited. You will have to pay a fee to send InMails beyond your allotted amount.

⊛ **Insights** – data collected about the visibility of your content and page.

⊛ **Interests** – shows your connections which companies or institutions you follow.

⊛ **Learning** – a massive and diverse platform of web-based training and educational programs.

⊛ **Notifications** – customizable feature which will get your attention when certain actions happen on LinkedIn. Remember that here, less is more.

- ⊛ **Premium** – LinkedIn Premium is a paid version of LinkedIn which adds a few perks and features.

- ⊛ **Profile** – your personal home page on LinkedIn. This should be public, polished, accurate, and complete.

- ⊛ **Publisher** – LinkedIn's built-in blog publishing software.

- ⊛ **Recommendation** – write and receive recommendations from colleagues, superiors, and coworkers through LinkedIn. Both the recommendations you receive and write for others will show up in your profile.

- ⊛ **Sales Navigator** – adds enhanced search and categorization tools for business and fund developers. A paid feature beyond the LinkedIn Premium expense.

- ⊛ **Skills & Endorsements** – a collection of skill keywords relevant to you and your industry. You can select which ones appear in your profile, and others can click to confirm your competency.

- ⊛ **Stories** – a single panel of content that disappears after twenty-four hours. If you're familiar with stories on Facebook, Instagram, or Snapchat, you'll be right at home. LinkedIn announced in August 2021 that it would be suspending the "Stories" feature effective September 30, 2021. They left the door open to bring an iteration of it back at some point, which is why I left it in here.

- ⊛ **Tagging** – mentioning another LinkedIn user or company in a post or comment to get their attention, give credit, or provide help. To tag, type @ and begin typing the name. A drop-down menu will eventually give you the option to select the person or company in question. Tagged entities will appear with a bolded blue text. The taggee will receive a notification that they have been tagged. This is an absolutely essential feature that should be used with the utmost discretion.

- ⊛ **Unfollow** – if you unfollow a connection, you'll remain connected, but their content will no longer show up in your feed. This is an integral part of your newsfeed curation, as it will prevent irrelevant or unpleasant content from being thrown at you on the regular.

MINDSET MATTERS

It's incredibly important to approach this journey with an open mind, a positive attitude, and the understanding that nothing will ever be "perfect." Your profile will never be perfect. Your content will never be perfect. Your approach to network and brand development will never be perfected. If you're waiting to achieve some standard or baseline before getting started . . . don't. Just don't. Instead, dive in. Scramble the eggs. Get messy. We'll worry about making a good-looking omelet later.

It's even more important to visualize remote networking through in-person goggles. As you engage with folks in comments and work to expand your network, ask yourself if you would approach the interaction in a similar fashion if you were face-to-face. If your answer is "no," then think twice.

Social media makes communicating a whole heck of a lot easier, and that can be a dangerous pitfall. For example, would you pitch coaching services to someone you just met or a stranger walking past you on the street? Would you get into a heated argument, call names, and threaten a complete stranger—as we so often see on Facebook and Twitter—as if you were standing there speaking to that person? Goodness, I sure hope not. Don't do it on LinkedIn either.

This whole undertaking may seem like a large endeavor. That's because it absolutely is—but the juice is worth the squeeze. The Department of Defense doesn't put a sincere effort into training its forces in professional network development prior to transition, and a network cannot be cultivated overnight. If it's true that our network is our net worth and that service members are given little to no encouragement or guidance developing a network prior to separation from the military, how likely is it that veterans will be able to achieve what they're capable of professionally?

A large, diverse, and organically developed network is a powerful thing. It is by far the key to success in post-service employment, entrepreneurship, and business development. It outweighs résumés, business cards, and degrees. By the time you finish this book, you should have the tools needed to build a polished LinkedIn presence, develop a powerhouse professional network on and off-line, and attain success in your career or entrepreneurial ambitions. In addition to having a full toolbox, I hope you'll walk away with a positive attitude and forward-thinking mindset.

Many of you are completely new to LinkedIn may not be particularly tech savvy or are playing catch-up in one way or another. The task set before you is a challenge, but one that's not at all insurmountable. Some of you are reading this book to sharpen your existing skills. You're in the right place too.

I'm committed to providing you with ongoing support. I'll do everything in my power to address your questions and point you in the right direction. Please feel free to connect with me on LinkedIn and any other social network. Each section of this book contains links with QR codes, like the one below, that lead to resources, support, and continuing education. See you at the end.

CHECK IT OUT!

I am committed to providing you with evergreen support. Click the link or scan the QR code to join my exclusive online community.

🌐 *https://community.adambraatz.com*

CHAPTER 4

LinkedIn Profile Essentials

John and Jack are veterans attending a business conference. They're both productive business developers looking for a change. They want new jobs with better hours, better benefits, and better pay. John is dressed in business casual with a fresh shave and a haircut. Jack is wearing camouflage pants, a tuxedo T-shirt, and hasn't showered in several days.

John approaches a prospective employer, shakes hands, makes eye contact, smiles, and says, "My name is John. It's a pleasure to meet you." Throughout the span of the brief conversation, John makes a good impression. He manages to tactfully insert his personal elevator pitch and share some of his experiences as well as express his overarching purpose in life. He lets some of his personality shine through. As the dialogue concludes, John extends an offer to have a further conversation about potential synergies between them, which is gladly accepted.

On the other end of the conference hall, Jack approaches a prospective employer as well, but he shakes hands so firmly he induces discomfort and stares into his prospect's soul with a furtive and intimidating glance. "I AM A VETERAN," he announces loudly without breaking eye contact.

His pursuit pulls his hand away and politely asks Jack about himself.

Without saying a word, Jack pulls out a résumé, squishes it into an unkempt wad, and throws it directly into the other man's face.

"What's your problem?" asks the man.

To which Jack replies robotically, "I am a seasoned, experienced professional with a proven history of leadership."

Shocked, the man looks at Jack with a quizzical expression. "Am I on a hidden camera or something? What's your name?"

"Project Manager," replies Jack blankly before he turns tail and sprints away, leaving the other man in confused silence.

Jack repeats this exact same process, as if it were cut-and-pasted, to every exhibitor in the conference center. He does not produce nor receive an ounce of value from this experience. When he gets home, Jack adds "Thought Leader" to his LinkedIn headline.

Sounds fairly ridiculous, doesn't it? Unfortunately, Jack was acting in real life the way many folks approach their interactions online. More specifically, Jack was the unfortunate personification of the way many veterans approach LinkedIn. Due to the comfort, convenience, and shielding from in-person social niceties on online platforms, we often forgo the customs and courtesies we extend when interacting face-to-face.

If you don't believe me, think about every time you've witnessed someone say something incredibly rude or threaten violence to a complete stranger on Facebook. Now consider the likelihood of that exchange occurring face-to-face.

Each platform has its own etiquette, too, which can lead to confusion. Many vets are guilty of treating LinkedIn like Twitter or Facebook while they're figuring things out, which is a huge problem. There are human beings on the other end of our social networks and digital platforms. It's important for us to frame our LinkedIn activities with that in mind, or our professional reputation and brand may suffer. It's also the right thing to do.

Many people have a reductive view of LinkedIn as simply a digital version of their own résumé. Sure, there are common threads between some sections of your LinkedIn profile and your résumé—your work experience, an executive summary, contact information, and recommendations—but LinkedIn is capable of much, much more. It's also different in several notable ways. Your LinkedIn profile is more like an atomic business card that's accessible 24/7 by any professional you hope to work for or with. It's a vehicle by which you can continuously express your expertise and value to your target audience. That said, similar to your résumé, you must have a clean, polished, and optimized LinkedIn landing page if you wish to convey your competence and expertise, and that is precisely where we'll start.

Your profile does not have to be 100% perfect before you unleash it on the world, but the quicker it achieves optimization the better. In other words, don't be afraid to dive in. But be prepared. You'll need to start swimming too. So what makes a LinkedIn profile "fully optimized?"

Visual completion. If your profile has incomplete or incorrectly done sections, the viewer will subconsciously perceive you as incomplete or incorrect. Would you hand over a half-finished résumé, a business card with errors, or respond to the question "tell me about yourself" with silence, or even worse, inappropriate language or bad grammar? Would you leave broken links or placeholder images on your business website? The perception of your competence and professionalism is largely dependent upon the quality and visual completion of your LinkedIn profile.

LINKEDIN PREMIUM AND PAID SERVICES

LinkedIn has free and paid plans available to the general public. The basic plan is free and allows you to use most of LinkedIn's most central features, though it occasionally limits certain aspects. Most people can get by with the free version. In fact, I've seen folks build businesses and huge platforms of influence with it. At $29.99, LinkedIn Premium gives you the most bang for your buck, boasting the following perks:

- ✴ additional inMail credits
- ✴ additional database searches
- ✴ the ability to see everyone who has viewed your profile
- ✴ unlimited access to LinkedIn Learning
- ✴ a gold Premium badge on your personal profile page

If you've been on LinkedIn for more than a few seconds, you've likely received some not-so-subtle encouragement to join LinkedIn Premium. Lucky for you as a veteran, you don't have to pay over $350 a year for access! As part of their ongoing commitment to our community, LinkedIn offers *free subscriptions* to LinkedIn Premium Career in one year increments for all service members and veterans, so the decision is a no-brainer as far as I'm concerned. But for those who are forced to pay for whatever reason, there are one month trials available so you can see which plan is right for you without any financial risk.

I get asked quite often whether or not I believe LinkedIn Premium to be a worthwhile investment. As is the case with much of my social media-related advice, the answer is, it depends. Overarchingly, I stand by my belief that nobody needs to pay for LinkedIn to build a powerful platform there. There are certain benefits that are worth their weight in gold, though, depending on your industry and goals.

Some argue that anyone on LinkedIn who is serious about what they're doing there—whether it be career, business, or platform development—must have the LinkedIn Premium badge on their profile. Give me a break. Personally, I've never looked at someone's standard profile and thought, "Not a Premium user? Seriously! What are they playing at? Make an effort!" And the implication that anyone does is foolish.

I don't use InMails very often but have found them to be exceptionally useful in network development a small handful of times. Having access to InMails for network development is like owning a big truck for towing and hauling lumber—super handy in theory, but if you only haul full sheets of plywood once a year, did you really need the truck, or could you have found another way to take care of business on the rare occasion you needed it?

Being able to see who's viewed your profile is a useful feature, if only because the alternative can lead to curiosity eating away at you. If you aren't paying for a Premium account, you'll have access to a tantalizing but incomplete view of who's been checking you out. Some people send connection requests to anyone who visits their page but, to me, that approach is like throwing a business card at anyone who looks at you on the street.

LinkedIn Learning is an incredibly useful tool. Its value cannot be overstated, especially if you find webinar-style education effective. You can find timely and valuable information about many topics from military transition to business and brand development to technical advice on software and more. Don't waste your free opportunity to dig into the treasure trove of information.

LinkedIn Sales Navigator is a lead generation and development pipeline tool that LinkedIn offers for a fairly hefty fee. I would advise that only certain people in very specific industries use this. If an employer requires it, they will most likely provide access. The average user, especially the military career transitioner, does not need Sales Navigator. The same goes for LinkedIn Recruiting Tools and Talent Solutions. If you aren't currently a recruiter whose employer uses this tool, you straight-up don't need it.

HOW TO GET A FREE PREMIUM SUBSCRIPTION

As I mentioned above, US military service members and veterans have access to a Premium Career Account for free. Eligible users will need to verify their service through ID.me. Most veterans will already be in the system, but if you haven't already set up your account, it only takes a couple of minutes.

I have found the language around whether or not this offer is only for one year to be intentionally vague. As you reach the end of your free Premium Subscription period, LinkedIn will ask for payment information so you don't have a lapse in service. If you'd like to continue to receive LinkedIn Premium Career for free, allow your free Premium Subscription to lapse without paying for an additional year. If you already have credit card information on file, you may need to actually cancel your account before the period ends in order to avoid being charged. Once your Premium Subscription ends, follow the above link again, and verify through ID.me. Boom! Yet another year of free Premium Career. You're welcome.

SETTINGS

Before populating your profile with information and images, head over to settings. In the upper righthand corner, you will see a box titled "Edit my custom URL," which is where we'll start. LinkedIn gives you the option of creating a custom URL that leads directly to your profile. By default, they provide you with a long line of numbers that would be impossible to remember. Ideally, your custom URL will be easier on the eyes and easier for everyone to remember. You can change it to something else later, but if you do so, remember to adjust any public redirect links, like from your website or other social accounts, accordingly.

I strongly advise making all your profile content visible and public. Though there are a number of ways to approach your presence on this platform, I still wouldn't put anything on LinkedIn that you wouldn't say or write in a semiprofessional setting. Folks can only access what you present to them, after all. Accordingly, there shouldn't be any risk involved in making your curated professional information public on LinkedIn.

The only exception would be the amount of contact information you set to be visible to 2nd and 3rd-degree connections—people outside of your network. On one hand, I would leave no barriers to someone being able to get in touch with you or see what you're all about. Having your email address visible publicly, however, does open you up to being added to mailing lists and the like against your wishes. It's a personal decision you must weigh out.

Head over to your profile, then click "Edit public profile & URL." On the mobile app, you would click the settings gear icon, then click "Visibility," then "Edit your public profile." This view shows what anyone in the general public, except people you've blocked, can see of your profile without being connected with you in any way. On the right side, you can toggle your profile's public visibility and select what information, if any, you want visible to 2nd and 3rd-degree connections.

The most highly debated setting is whether or not to have your profile picture visible to nonconnections. If your visibility's limited, people outside of your network will not be able to see your profile picture or full name, which decreases the likelihood that they'll connect or engage with you. Folks may see you in the comments section of one of their connection's posts and decline the urge to connect with you because you have a generic

---

32

photo and incomplete name. Some believe that these accounts look like scam accounts or are otherwise untrustworthy.

I have everything set to visible and strongly suggest you do the same. At a minimum, your full name and profile picture should be visible to the public. You may want to hide certain things in some circumstances. I once coached a client who sought to avoid any contact from an ex-spouse and made her full name and profile picture accessible only to 1st-degree connections. Totally understandable. Again, it's a personal decision.

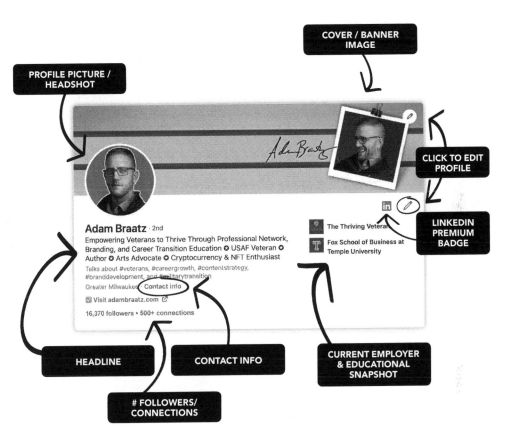

Take a moment to dig into your notification settings. LinkedIn's default notification settings are enough to drive anyone insane. You definitely don't need to be receiving emails or push notifications every time one of your connections sneezes. Trust me, you're better off without that nonsense, and taking a few minutes to turn most of the notifications off will save you more than a few headaches and lots of time down the road.

YOUR NAME

Before populating your profile with information and images, head over to settings. In thThis seems like a no-brainer, but it must be said because I've unfortunately come across this a handful of times. Use whatever first and last name on your profile that you would use on a résumé or in a professional setting. Spell it correctly and use capitalization, for Pete's sake. Currently, you're allowed 20 characters for a first name and 40 for a last name.

CHECK IT OUT!

If you have a former name or commonly used a nickname, you can add that to your profile, which may be extremely valuable for people who knew you by a different name or before a name change due to marriage, divorce, or similar circumstances.

https://www.linkedin.com/help/linkedin/answer/1288/former-or-maiden-name-on-your-profile

I've seen many people try to garner attention by putting emojis in their names, and I can sympathize with the temptation. In fact, I used to advise others to put an emoji before their first name in order to discern when a potential connection was reaching out via automation. For example, since my name was listed as ✪ Adam Braatz ✪, an automated message would begin with a salutation like "Hello ✪," or "Good morning ✪." Then I would know not to connect with whoever sent the message because they were using a bot and clearly didn't genuinely care about me or our connection.

Unfortunately, automators got wise to the tactic and made some easy tweaks to their programs that left out non-alphanumeric characters. More importantly, I learned that having anything other than your first and last name listed can impede the search function. That means that if someone tries to search for you or tag you in a post, you may not pop up right away unless they remember the exact emoji that precedes your name and lead with that. You don't want to create any speedbumps to being found or tagged by others, so leave the emojis out of your name.

If you have a former name or nickname, you can add that as well, which may be extremely valuable for people who knew you by a different name or before a name change due to marriage, divorce, or similar circumstances.

YOUR PROFILE PICTURE

Your profile picture is arguably the most important part of your profile and overall presence on LinkedIn. This picture shows up next to every post and comment you make. It's the first thing potential connections, employers, and business partners will see. It's your instant, automatic nonverbal elevator pitch.

Many veterans use their most recent headshot from military service, looking stern and polished in their freshly starched dress uniform. That's what I did.

See the adjacent photo, which can also be found in the encyclopedia under the word "Merica."

Now that I know better, I advise strongly against doing this for a number of reasons, though I can sympathize with the thought process. Shouldn't a potential employer see and perceive excellence, professionalism, resiliency, loyalty, and leadership? In theory, yes. In reality, no. Most don't. The whole militaristic vibe and all the unfortunate conscious and subconscious stereotypes about veterans that accompany it are what come to mind for most civilian hiring authorities and potential connections.

Many civilians are scared of you in one way or another, whether they want to admit it or not. They fear what they don't understand or have personal experience with. According to the Pew Research Center, the percentage of Americans who either serve or have family members who serve is lower than ever and has been on a near-continuous decline since the phasing out of the draft in the midseventies. This means that there is an ever-shrinking societal basis of collective understanding about our entire community.

Either you are no longer in the military or will transition someday, so you need to start looking to the future. You've likely heard the cliché "dress for the job you want." Well, you aren't applying to be a staff sergeant or colonel in the civilian workplace. Whether your transition is two months or twenty years away doesn't matter. You should be focused on developing your network to prepare for your future beyond the military, and your profile must reflect that.

Additionally, people rarely smile in their military headshots. I sure didn't. I wanted to look as polished and formidable as possible. Numerous studies show, however, that potential employers, clients, and business partners are more likely to view you as competent and worth engaging with if you're smiling in your headshot. Show off those pearly whites, and if that's too much of a stretch for you, at least do your best to avoid looking as if you're about to give someone wall-to-wall counseling.

I don't make a habit of encouraging folks to go out and spend money. Your military transition can be a financially trying time, and I take recommendations to cough up awfully seriously. That said, I advise that you invest in a professional portrait. A single headshot with a real-deal professional portrait photographer could easily cost you over $300, but you won't regret that investment. If paying for a headshot isn't in the cards right now, you can take a decent photo on any relatively modern smartphone. Many even have a portrait mode that is built specifically for that type of endeavor.

If you're doing the picture yourself, remember the following:

- ✱ Enlist a reliable friend or family member to help if possible. This is much too important a task to entrust to your multitasking selfie skills.

- ✱ Dress for the job you want. Minimally, I suggest a blouse or collared shirt.

- ✱ Don't stand with your back flat against a wall. Your headshot could end up looking more like a mugshot. Angling slightly works wonders.

- ✱ Capture your head and shoulders. No need for a full-length shot.

- ✱ Leave a little bit of room on either side and above you. LinkedIn allows for a square photo, but then throws a circular frame around it. You'll be able to zoom and crop as necessary, but if your headshot is too much of a closeup, the circular frame may cut parts of you off.

- ✱ Ensure that you have ample lighting—as much of it as possible. If you don't have enough light or all the light is coming from a single direction, you run the risk of creating some creepy looking shadows.

- ✱ Stand in front of a backdrop with a mild, solid color that contrasts with the color of your clothing. Avoid overactive patterns.

- ✱ Look at the camera and *smile*. Don't be bashful. Let 'er flicker.

If you have an existing portrait on hand that checks all the boxes above, then you can always roll with that. Keep in mind, however, that the picture should be recent—taken within the last few years. I'm sure you looked spectacular in your Glamour Shot from 1994, but your LinkedIn profile picture should look like you today.

If you like how your photo turned out but don't much care for the background, or if you feel it could be a bit more bright or cheerful, you can easily edit it after the fact. I use Canva to do exactly that. I remove the background and replace it with a light gradient that makes my photo really stand out. You don't have to be exceptionally tech savvy to make this happen. I'm not a digital asset editor or designer by any means, so if I can do it, so can you. Canva is easy as pie.

CHECK IT OUT!

Making your headshot pop on your profile is simple using Canva. Learn how with this quick tutorial video:

 https://canvatutorial.adambraatz.com

COVER IMAGE / BANNER

In both mobile and desktop applications, LinkedIn allows for a large backdrop photo to reside at the top of your profile. This is known as a cover, banner, or background photo. LinkedIn will automatically populate that space with a generic space-filler. Nothing says "I don't care very much about my profile" more than leaving the default up. If you click on the pencil icon to edit the banner photo, LinkedIn will offer a few options to replace the generic space-filler. If any of them speak to you, go for it.

It can be a challenge to find content for your banner that fits — literally and figuratively. LinkedIn suggests an image size of 1584 x 396, but many users find it challenging to convey who they are or what they do in that size space. Too often, I see folks add text, links, and logos to their banner photos. Be very careful with this approach — you want to avoid having your background photo look like an amusement park billboard.

If you're not sure what to put in, I suggest using a cityscape. Make sure the picture is high resolution (hi-res) and of a location you're hoping to be employed in or the nearest metropolitan area to it. That way, a potential connection visiting your profile may see your banner and think, Hey, I've been there! Or subconsciously feel a connection with you because of your shared residency.

Your banner image and the way it sits behind your profile picture are different between your desktop and mobile app. After you upload, adjust, crop, and zoom your profile and banner photos to perfection on desktop, make sure to check it out on mobile or vice versa. The formatting could look great on one, but not on the other. It often takes tweaking, especially if you're risking the billboard approach. My favorite way to easily fix the formatting, resizing, cropping, and minor editing is by using Canva. Check out the link below for more information, and remember, a vast majority of Canva's features are *free*.

CHECK IT OUT!

I'm a huge fan of Canva and use it just about every day to create graphic designs, simple videos, or edit photos. It is an absolutely essential tool in your toolbox, and it's super easy to use!

*The best news is that a majority of its features are available in the **free** version. Sign up here:*

🌐 **https://partner.canva.com/adambraatz**

CHAPTER 5

The Headline

Your headline is the area of text directly beneath your name that shows up in your profile — and beside your profile picture — on posts and comments. This section is the most neglected and misused. Aside from your profile picture, it's also the most important.

LinkedIn doesn't adequately convey the immense opportunity that your headline presents. Your headline will default to read *job title* at *employer*. If you change it to something more creative, they will ask — frequently — if you'd like to change it back. Don't take the bait. This chunk of text shows up next to nearly every single thing you do on this platform, and we are encouraged to squander the chance to share something about what we do, how we do it, why we do it, or who we serve in lieu of *Project Manager at BoringCompany* or some nonsense? Good grief.

Your headline is a 220-character elevator pitch. Think about how you'd respond if someone asked, "How can you bring value to me or my company?" Or "Why should I connect with you?" Replying with, "ME PROJECT MANAGER" or the equivalent wouldn't exactly tell the whole story, nor would it impress anyone. After all, not all project managers are created equal, and you are more than your job title.

BUILDING YOUR HEADLINE: THE ATTENTION GRABBER

I prefer to view headlines as if they were split into two separate sections. First, you have an attention-grabbing sentence that concisely and powerfully conveys what you bring to the table. Not long ago, there was a headline formula parroted by LinkedIn influencers which is no longer in vogue, but I still believe it's a great place to start when brainstorming your attention grabber. Are you ready? Here it is:

I help ____ do ____ by/with/through ____.

Starting with this formula will get you in the right mindset. Who do you endeavor to serve? What will you help them do, accomplish, or overcome? In what way will you do it?

38

You may need to think outside the box in some circumstances, but it works for literally any profession.

Pretend you're a salesperson at a shoe store in Boston, Massachusetts. Though your interaction with a customer may end at the point of sale, consider the larger picture. What is the end result of a satisfied customer finding an affordable shoe that is both fashionable and a perfect fit? Comfort. Confidence. Health. Rather than Shoe Salesperson at Foot Factory, your headline could read I Help Bostonians Discover Comfort Through Modern Footwear. Or perhaps, I Help Boston Walk Farther and Run Faster. There are a million better ways to express the bigger picture of your impact in the world than Shoe Salesperson at Foot Factory.

In the above examples, please take note of how I used capitalization as if I were writing the title of a blog, article, or book. I would definitely advise doing the same, but if you elect to take a different approach, be consistent. Capitalization inconsistencies come off as lazy mistakes.

As I mentioned above, using this formula is an important place to begin your headline journey, but you're still a few steps away from a truly polished and compelling headline. The above examples are a bit long, clunky, and use some pretty flaccid verbiage. Let's take these examples to the next level:

I Help Bostonians Find Comfort Through Modern Footwear.

"Help" is not powerful enough. Nor is "find." Look for stronger power words. Thesaurus.com is your friend here. But watch out not to go over the top with pretentious or excessively uncommon words.

I Empower Bostonians to Discover Comfort Through Modern Footwear.

What kind of Bostonians do you empower? This is a great opportunity to throw in a sly compliment to your discerning target audience.

What kind of comfort? To what extent? Are your satisfied customers experiencing ho-hum comfort or comfort that will absolutely blow their minds? We want people to picture transcendental levels of comfort.

I Empower Fashion-Minded Bostonians to Discover Next-Level Comfort Through Modern Footwear.

"Through Modern Footwear" leaves nothing to the imagination, and it doesn't explain how or in what way you do what you do. If it isn't specific or valuable, change it or cut it off.

> **I Empower Fashion-Minded Bostonians to Discover Next-Level Comfort.**
>
> Or if you sell athletic shoes, try this.

> **I Empower Fitness-Focused Bostonians to Walk Farther and Run Faster.**

There are a billion ways to customize your headline statement to fit your personality and industry. Take time to tweak it and try out different power words, then upload the headline to your profile. It doesn't have to be 100% perfect, and I encourage you to allow it to evolve naturally over time. I make at least a small change to my headline weekly.

BUILDING YOUR HEADLINE: HODGEPODGE

I call the headline content that comes after your attention grabber "hodgepodge." During this section, you use keywords that further explain things that you are capable of, certified in, or have a strong connection with. You can also show a bit of your personality here. It's common to separate these different keywords and ideas with a vertical line (|) or a symbol of some kind. Which you use is up to you.

The keywords in your headline are important. They not only help a viewer zero in on what you're all about or develop interest in what you have to offer, they're also used in database searches by potential connections, customers, business partners, or employers. For example, if you aspire to become a project manager after service and are holding a Project Management Professional (PMP) certification, then you should include that in the hodgepodge section. I also suggest putting your branch of service in there. Remember, you have 220 characters to work with, but you definitely don't need to use them all. In most formats, especially on mobile, content beyond the first line will be cut off with an ellipsis anyway.

Using our favorite shoe salesperson as an example:

> **I Empower Fitness-Focused Bostonians to Walk Farther and Run Faster | PMP Certified | US Army Veteran | CrossFit Enthusiast |**
>
> It has become acceptable, heck, even common, to use an emoji or two in your headline. As always, I suggest keeping things simple in order to avoid looking like a billboard. The last thing you want is over-the-top, sleazy, snake oil salesperson vibes. The above example could use an emoji. A shoe would be apropos.

> 👟 **I Empower Fitness-Focused Bostonians to Walk Farther and Run Faster | PMP Certified | US Army Veteran | CrossFit Enthusiast |**

I find that leading with an emoji is effective—just ONE emoji, please, not a row of them. But keep in mind that an emoji can look visually confusing when followed by an "I" statement. For this reason, I suggest changing the tense of your attention grabber away from first-person narrative. In this instance, the "I" statement could appear as if the shoe is claiming to do the empowering.

> 👟 **Empowering Fitness-Focused Bostonians to Walk Farther and Run Faster | PMP Certified | US Army Veteran | CrossFit Enthusiast |**

Here's an example of taking out the "I" statement.

> 👟 **Empowering Fitness-Focused Bostonians to Walk Farther and Run Faster ⊛ PMP Certified ⊛ US Army Veteran ⊛ CrossFit Enthusiast ⊛**

Once you have your headline relatively squared away, it's time to verify the visual formatting, like you did with your profile and banner photos. Your headline may look lovely on your desktop browser, but the formatting may look weird via mobile. If this is the case, experiment with rearranging the order of your hodgepodge items or rephrasing them. Move or remove emojis and symbols. If you have a "personality item" in your hodgepodge—I've seen folks write Dog Dad or even Guitar Hero—I suggest leaving it for the very end.

HEADLINES FOR CAREER TRANSITIONERS

If you're about to face a career transition, are in the process of separating or retiring from military service, or are aspiring to switch careers after service, you must take special care with your headline. In a similar vein to "dress for the job you want," your headline should express your capabilities and value proposition for the industry to which you aspire to transition. The process of finding the parallels between your current position and finding the future requirements in a civilian workplace is colloquially referred to as "translating your skills," which is an infuriatingly misunderstood cliché.

Whatever we call it, military folks often see this process as challenging, and understandably so. Many military jobs and career fields don't have logical civilian counterparts and feel awfully distant from the civilian workplace on the whole. What on earth would a munitions specialist who aspires to work in marketing, for example, put in their headline?

Hardly. We're trying hard not to scare potential civilian employers and connections here. The key is to find common threads between where you are and where you wish to be. Start at a tactical level and gradually work toward strategic commonalities as needed. Consider this the nonmathematical equivalent of finding the lowest common denominator. At the most tactical level, a marketing specialist may write copy and manage a brand's social platforms, while a munitions specialist transports ammunition to the front lines. At the most strategic level, both are jobs and require the participant to be alive and breathing.

In between those poles, it's not unrealistic to suggest that both positions would be responsible for project deliverables and resource logistics, which is where you could focus in this instance. Start at the bottom with the tactical and work your way to more strategic objectives until you've found commonality. Here are some examples:

	Munitions Specialist	Marketing Manager
Tactical (Not Related)	transports ammunition to frontline fighters	writes copy, replies to customer inquiries, manages social media
Getting Closer	supports combat operations that inspire things and people to break	supplies content that inspires consumers to buy products
BINGO!	oversees campaign resource logistics	oversees project resource logistics
Vague	supports mission accomplishment	supports project deliverables
Strategic (Too Broad)	alive and breathing	alive and breathing

Sometimes, the common denominator will simply be too broad. Don't sweat it. As your experience, education, and accomplishments grow in your new chosen field, your headline will evolve to become more specific. Our marketing-minded munitions professional could begin with a headline that looks something like this:

| Employ Explosive Methods to Inspire Audience Behavior | Campaign Logistics | Precision Competition Disruption | US Army Veteran | Broadway Superfan 🎭

Some common denominators may feel less common and more like a semantic stretch. There's definitely a delicate balance to maintain. Don't do anything you aren't comfortable with, don't stretch the truth, and don't fabricate your experience or abilities. If what you're saying, especially in your headline, makes you feel uncomfortable, go with your gut and zoom out to a more strategic commonality.

There are millions of variables to putz with, and there are trends that will invariably go in and out of fashion. LinkedIn may decide to disallow emojis in headlines someday. They could shorten or lengthen the number of characters you have to work with at any time, without notice. We must view our headline as an ever-evolving, adaptable, living element.

I thoroughly enjoy workshopping headlines. I've been known to spend over an hour on a virtual chat with clients brainstorming and piecing them together. It's important to spend an ample amount of time because they're really, really important. Don't rush through your development process. If executed correctly, a great headline can inspire people to connect with you, do business with you, purchase from you, or hire you. Below is an example of a quality headline and an upper profile area transformation:

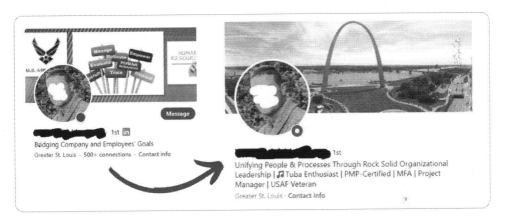

CHAPTER 6

━━ ⭐ ━━

The Rest of Your LinkedIn Profile

CONTACT INFORMATION

Your header section includes a linked text for "Contact Info." You have a modicum of control over what shows up when connections or general LinkedIn users click on it. Generally speaking, I would advise that you make sure there are no barriers to get in touch with you. That said, having your personal contact information visible does make you vulnerable to Internet crazies.

In 2022, LinkedIn added the option to place a link in the main heading section of your profile. You can select any external link and customize the text that will appear. Be very cautious here, as people will see and click on this link. Ensure that wherever your visitors end up is polished and professional. If your website is under construction, you're better off without any link at all. Additionally, don't put a link here that you don't want to represent you fully. If you're hunting for a job in cybersecurity, for example, sharing a link to your athletic supplement multilevel marketing side hustle in your main section is not a good idea.

While it is advisable to have most or all of your LinkedIn content visible to the public in most circumstances, it is a personal decision to do so. There are some situations where it isn't smart or safe to do so. Use your best discretion.

This advice is of particular importance when it comes to your contact information.

As a general rule, never write or post anything on the internet that you aren't comfortable with the world seeing.

THE DASHBOARD

Your dashboard gives you quick and convenient access to a number of LinkedIn features and analytics. As of this writing, the dashboard has been split into two separate sections: analytics and resources. Regardless of what this section is called, it resides directly underneath your top profile segment. You are the only one who can view your personal dashboard, resources, and analytics.

Your dashboard shows how many people have viewed your profile in the past ninety days, how many times your original content has been seen or engaged with in the last week—also called impressions—and how many times you've appeared in a LinkedIn search during the previous week. If you have a LinkedIn Premium Subscription, clicking on the number of profile views will bring you to a page with more data and list exactly who's viewed your profile and when. This is something incredibly important to bear in mind. Most people will be able to see that you've viewed their profile. LinkedIn is the only major platform that has a feature like that built into it.

You can turn this feature off and stay hidden as you browse other profiles. Some people choose to do this for privacy reasons. I should warn you that doing so will also restrict your features and ability to see the very information on someone else's profile that you're trying to hide on yours.

Your dashboard will also show how many content views your most recent post or article has received and how many times you've shown up on a database search by other LinkedIn users. Clicking on either number will give you more detailed information about both areas. Depending on whether or not you meet certain criteria, you'll have the option to turn on "Creator Mode," which rearranges your profile to feature your original content more prominently than anything else. If you're just getting started or are early in your LinkedIn journey, you can skip "Creator Mode." The jury's still out as to whether or not there's any measurable benefit. I've heard conflicting reports from various influencers on the platform. I have "Creator Mode" turned on but, honestly, I haven't seen much of a difference. That said, LinkedIn has been devoting an abundance of resources to developing their creator support programs. We'll see what they come out with in the near future.

Those with "Creator Mode" turned on will also have the "Follow" button featured on their profile page rather than a button that says "Connect." You can still connect with a creator by clicking the "More" button. The opposite is true for the non-creators who have the "Connect" button featured on their profile page. If you'd prefer to follow them instead of sending a full-blown connection request, the "More" button has what you're looking for. If you want to expand your connections first and foremost, this is an important consideration. It may be hard to believe, but having a "Follow" button on your main profile can be a turnoff for folks who would otherwise have clicked "Connect" without hesitation.

Creators also have access to a "Creator Hub," which gives them the option to select five hashtags to display at the top of their profile. In theory, this will give visitors an idea what you like to talk about to help them decide whether or not to follow you. The "Creator Hub" will also let you know if you have authorization to create content through LinkedIn Live or the Newsletter feature.

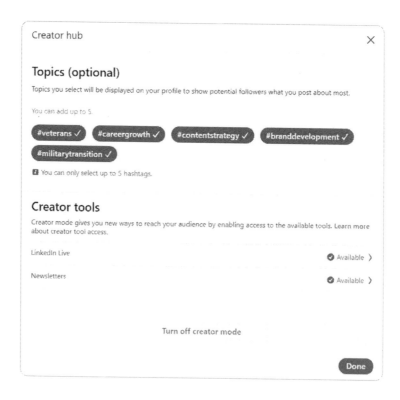

Right above this area, you'll also be able to turn on what I lovingly refer to as "The Beacon." I'm including it here because it used to be located in the dashboard, and in my humble opinion, I believe that it was better placed there. You can now access the option by clicking the "Open To" button on the bottom of your main profile section. This lets your entire network aware that you're open to work. More specifically, it makes you visible to recruiters based on their keyword database searches.

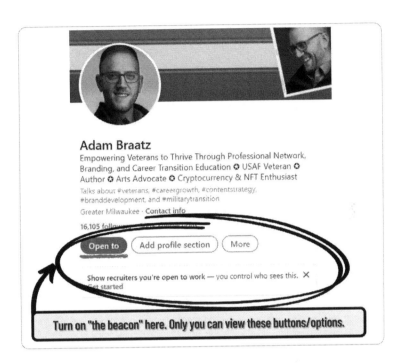

You can specify which job titles, locations, and other details you require. If you don't want your current employer to know you're looking for other work but still want recruiters to be able to find you, make sure you click the appropriate toggle before publishing. If you're looking for work or are on the heels of a transition, I would definitely suggest having it on. The efficacy and frequency of employment via recruiter varies widely from industry to industry, but it will never hurt. As to whether or not you want an #opentowork badge to appear on your public profile picture, well, that's up to you! Some believe it comes off as desperate, while others swear by it.

FEATURED CONTENT

When other LinkedIn users visit your profile, the section containing your profile picture and headline will always be the first thing they see. What's visible directly below that depends upon whether or not you have "Creator Mode" on and which sections are populated with content or set to be visible. Though many of you will have the "About" section directly under your headline, I'll dive into "Featured Content" next.

You can choose which content appears in the "Featured Content" section. You can feature posts, articles, external links, and media. You should do all of the above, if only in the spirit of visual completion. If you have original content, articles, blogs, awards, or have been mentioned in a publication of any kind, this is where you can share it—and you absolutely should.

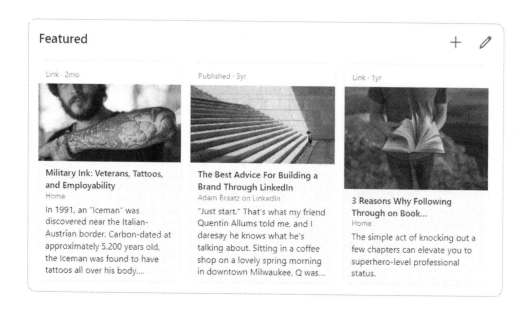

Featured   +   ✏

Link · 2mo

Military Ink: Veterans, Tattoos, and Employability
Home
In 1991, an "Iceman" was discovered near the Italian-Austrian border. Carbon-dated at approximately 5,200 years old, the Iceman was found to have tattoos all over his body....

Published · 3yr

The Best Advice For Building a Brand Through LinkedIn
Adam Braatz on LinkedIn
"Just start." That's what my friend Quentin Allums told me, and I daresay he knows what he's talking about. Sitting in a coffee shop on a lovely spring morning in downtown Milwaukee, Q was...

Link · 1yr

3 Reasons Why Following Through on Book...
Home
The simple act of knocking out a few chapters can elevate you to superhero-level professional status.

No need to share your life's work in this space. As visitors scroll by, the most they'll be able to see without hitting the arrow that reveals more is three pieces of featured content. On mobile, it's more like one and a half. If your content or link doesn't have a preview photo attached to it or if the preview photo is formatted oddly or of a low resolution, don't share it in this section. The preview photos auto-populate based on the link and, as of this writing, can't be changed. LinkedIn, if you're listening, allowing folks to change the preview image for external links would be totally clutch. Be a pal.

Remember, *visual completion* has priority. I don't care if the article is the greatest thing you or anybody has ever written in the history of all of humankind. If the image attached to it's a pixelated mess, it will do significantly more harm to your professional presentation than anything else. Don't skip this section either—even if you haven't dedicated time to creating or curating content like blog articles or posts. Have you worked with a team or crew that's accomplished something that was written about in a post or article? Did you participate in a volunteer project that was written about somewhere online? Did you receive a trophy in your college debate club and have your name listed in the university digital newsletter? As long as the preview picture attached to it is pretty to look at, that's all good stuff.

I've seen many people, especially veterans, post their résumés in this section, and it's to their detriment. Don't do it. First, it looks desperate and tacky. Second, your résumé should be customized for each position you apply for. A recruiter may decline to reach out to you after stumbling upon your generic résumé if it doesn't fit the position they're looking to fill. This would be a crying shame, especially if a specifically curated résumé from you would have grabbed their attention.

If you can't find anything like the above to share in your "Featured Content" section, consider the following: are there any articles that convey an opinion you share about the industry you're in or headed toward? Does your current employer or unit have a web page with a mission or vision statement or one that outlines a project you're participating in? The possibilities are endless.

If you don't have any of that, you'll have to create share-worthy content yourself. One of the most effective items you can put in here is an original blog article. Luckily, the process is much easier than you would think thanks to a little known but powerful tool LinkedIn has up its sleeve. No worries if you don't have a blog page or website. Friends, LinkedIn has a built-in publisher. We'll get into that in depth in the "Content Creation" section.

THE ABOUT SECTION

I've seen some pretty horrendous "About" sections. Before I get into how to build a great "About" section, I want to establish some important ground rules:

⊛ Your "About" section is an opportunity to talk about your "why," what makes you tick, and your purpose in life. It should be personal yet professional.

⊛ Readers should walk away with an understanding of who you are as a person and as a professional.

⊛ You have 2000 characters to work with. Use them.

⊛ I strongly recommend writing in the first person rather than the third person. "I" versus "he."

⊛ This is not an executive summary. You don't need to talk about your experience or work history in this area. Your work history and experience will be outlined in detail in a later section of your profile.

⊛ No fluff words allowed. About 90% of new military transitioners start this section with a completely useless and asinine fluff word. In fact, if I had a dollar for every "About" section I've seen that started with "Experienced leader with a demonstrated ability," I'd be a very rich man. *Experienced?* Your experience section should show that you're experienced. *Proven?* Let your work prove that you're proven. Same goes for *demonstrated ability.* Yikes. *Seasoned?* As a friend of mine once asked me, "What are you, a steak?"

⊛ "Leader" is not a job title or position in the civilian workforce.

⊛ Being able to "multitask" is not a flex.

Look, I'm not trying to be a curmudgeon about this. I'm definitely not judging. I've made just about every mistake in the book with my "About" section. In fact, I created the world's worst executive summary on my first post-service résumé and then copied it verbatim into my LinkedIn "About" section. It stayed that way for months. Double yikes. When I say the world's worst executive summary, I mean it. See for yourself:

Experienced marketer, social networking representative, public affairs ambassador, producer, and program facilitator seeking a position as _____. Specializes in operations management, logistics, curriculum development, community and media relations, web marketing, and event planning. Personable team player, adept leader, sagacious multitasker, and avid learner with exceptional written and verbal communication skills, superb technological competence, and over 8 years of experience with web-based and social network marketing.

A few notes on the above:

⊛ I started with a fluff word: *Experienced.*

⊛ I listed eleven specialties. Can anyone truly *specialize* in that many things? The answer is no.

⊛ *SAGACIOUS MULTITASKER?* *facepalm*

⊛ Notice how pompous and robotic the whole thing is. It almost sounds as if I dug into a thesaurus in an attempt to find the most impressive-sounding words — because that is exactly what I did. *double facepalm*

Now that we've established what to avoid in your "About" section and—as an added bonus—in your résumé's executive summary, we can get into what makes a good "About" section. Consider what a visitor is looking for when they happen upon this section. Anyone reading it will be trying to glean insights about who you are and what drives you forward, personally and professionally.

If you decide on writing in the first person—and again, I strongly suggest you do—you'll have to experiment with the overall tone to make sure you sound like yourself. In addition to tone, your purpose is also highly individual. Here's what my personal about section looks like as of this writing:

Hello! My name is Adam Braatz (pronounced "brats" as in multiple German sausages.)

I'm a family man, veteran, author, entrepreneur, geriatric millennial, and reluctant DIY enthusiast. I am, and have always been, an educator at heart. My purpose lies in helping others overcome obstacles, grow, and realize the joy of unleashing their true potential.

This enduring purpose has manifested into a truly diverse, interdisciplinary career. I'm thankful for each and every adventure and the incredible professionals I've met along the way. The common thread throughout my wide range of experiences is a passion for empowering those in need.

Don't be bashful—I'm here to help!

Notice that *purpose* is the central theme. Author and world-famous inspirational speaker Simon Sinek would call it your "why." As far as your "About" section goes, people don't care if you're an actuary with ten years of experience. Save that brand of technical detail for your "Experience" section. Your "About" section should be more about what drives you, propels you forward, and makes you tick. Now if an actuary saved you from a burning building when you were a child and inspired in you a lifelong desire to fulfill your destiny as an actuary, then you're in business. Share that.

In a rare convenient twist, career transitioners have an advantage in this regard. Your purpose, or why, is the highest common denominator that motivates all your earthly endeavors. It usually doesn't matter how disparate your future career field or industry feels from your current job. Modern professionals may change jobs frequently, but your purpose is fundamental to who you and likely won't change often, if at all. In other words, wherever you are in your career transition journey, you should be able to fill this section out.

Notice that I also put my personality out there in its full glory while simultaneously mitigating a common mispronunciation issue. Whatever your personality or general mood is, this is the time to celebrate it. Let 'er rip.

HYBRID CONSIDERATIONS

Be on the lookout for ways to repurpose material from your profile and original content. You don't need to generate completely original stuff for every section and every platform.

The real-life equivalent would be buying a great outfit and only wearing it once. You should try to get the most mileage possible out of all your content.

Here are a few examples of ways you can repurpose content from your LinkedIn profile:

Headline – *Use in your Twitter/Instagram bio or in-person elevator pitch.*

About Section – *Tweak to use in resume executive summary.*

Recommendations – *With permission, use quotes on website & socials.*

Activity – *All original content can be posted elsewhere (with tweaks).*

The possibilities are endless — don't treat your content like a single-use item. Coffee mugs, not paper cups.

ACTIVITY

The "Activity" section shows how many followers a user has and how they've engaged with others on the platform recently. Clicking on "See All Activity" shows you just that—all that user's LinkedIn activity. Posts, comments, likes, articles, documents, you name it. This is a valuable tool if you're trying to glean information from others but dangerous if you aren't being smart with how you use the platform.

Other users can view the content that you post and engage with in this section. Connections, business partners, employees, employers, everyone. We'll get into avoiding controversial or polarizing topics in a later section. As a general rule, don't post anything that you wouldn't say in a professional environment. I acknowledge that I've said that before. It bears repeating. Additionally, don't like or comment on something that wouldn't be appropriate in a professional environment either. Many people avoid posting original content featuring polarizing subjects but don't consider that folks will also see when they click the thumbs up on that same type of material. Both can be a turnoff for a potential connection.

YOUR EXPERIENCE SECTION

Your "Experience" section is will most closely mirror the bulk of your résumé. In fact, I advise that you start populating this area by yanking bullet points from your résumé. This is the only occasion when I'll tell you to simply cut and paste from your performance report bullets and résumé highlights. If you don't have bullets or highlights—fairly common for whatever position you're currently holding, especially if you're relatively new to it—write a paragraph narrative about the mission and impact of the organization and what you do for it. A few considerations:

- ✴ You have 2000 characters to work with for each position in your "Experience" section.

- ✴ When you enter your place of employment, make sure you select a company page from the drop-down menu. All the major branches of the military have a company page on LinkedIn.

- ✴ Ensure that your start and end dates are accurate.

- ✴ Your military job titles can be "civilianized" a bit. For example, I wrote "Education and Training Manager" instead of "Military Training Instructor" or "Drill Instructor."

- ✴ Avoid military shorthand and acronyms like the plague. I see them pop up in this section more than any other, and most people don't have a clue what *any* of them mean.

- ✴ As with your résumé, keywords and data that represent the impact of what you've accomplished give you much more mileage.

- ✴ Each job in your "Experience" section can be adorned with supporting media. At the very bottom of the "Edit Experience" popup, you can add media or external links. As with your "Featured Content" section, visual completion is the priority here. If you don't have anything specific, the company's website or "About Us" section works rather well, so long as the preview photo comes through and isn't blurry.

- ✴ Should you include your first job from back when you worked at the Dollar Bucket in high school? It depends. Generally speaking, there's no need to go back *that* far unless there's a specific connection to that position and where you aspire to be career-wise.

EDUCATION, LICENSES, & CERTIFICATIONS

The "Education" section is relatively self-explanatory. That said, your intro section at the top of your profile will default to display whatever educational institution you have at the top of your list in the education section. You can reorder your education history regardless of start and end dates at your discretion by clicking and dragging the three lines under the pencil icon on the right side. Whatever you drag to the top of that section will show in your main profile box at the top of your profile.

There's a chance you may have heard the adage "skills are king," as it pertains to the civilian workforce. It's absolutely true. If you have certifications in anything, list them here.

VOLUNTEER EXPERIENCE

Most military members have volunteered at one time or another. Don't skip this section, as it serves two important purposes. It adds to the overall level of visual completion of your profile and also helps people understand what makes you tick. If you want to discover what's truly important to someone, check out what they do with their time when they aren't getting paid. If you're a business or fund developer of any kind, this is essential information as you develop prospects for sales pitches and the like.

SKILLS AND ENDORSEMENTS

Truth be told, I've not found this section to be valuable. I find it to be more annoying than anything else. That said, I have heard that recruiters in certain industries often use this section to narrow down potential acquisitions. Having it filled out will never hurt you, so it's best to knock it out.

Take LinkedIn's skill quiz or write your own skill keywords in this section. As time goes on, your connections will endorse certain skills and attributes they've witnessed in you. One of the best ways to encourage others to endorse the skills you claim is to do an exchange. Endorse others, and they'll often endorse you back.

 HYBRID CONSIDERATIONS

Your LinkedIn "Recommendations" can (and should) be repurposed as quality endorsements on your website or other platforms.

It's common courtesy to ask for your recommender's permission before using it elsewhere first.

RECOMMENDATIONS

Your "Recommendations" section is immensely more valuable than "Skills and Endorsements." In order to populate this area, I suggest taking a similar approach. Do an exchange. Recommend a friend, client, boss, or colleague and then request they do the same. You can request a recommendation from a connection by clicking the "More" button in their profile intro section, then "Request a recommendation."

Recommendations require more of a narrative approach. Take the recommendations you write seriously, and you'll usually be paid back in kind. In fact, if you focus first and foremost on being a giver on this platform, the "LinkedIn Karma Spirits" will typically take care of you.

Check out the following handy checklist for a breakdown of all the things you need to put together for a complete profile. Now that your profile's relatively polished, we can talk about building your digital professional network and leveraging LinkedIn's massive and powerful database to gain fruitful connections.

INITIAL PROFILE SETUP CHECKLIST

☐ My settings are adjusted to ensure public visibility.

☐ My profile picture is high quality. I'm wearing civilian professional attire and smiling.

☐ My banner/background photo is high resolution, relevant, and not too busy.

☐ Both my profile and banner pictures are formatted correctly on both desktop and mobile applications. I've checked!

☐ My headline is optimized, conveys the impact I have, and is not generic.

☐ I have verified my contact information.

☐ I have activated my "Open To Work" beacon (where applicable).

☐ I have at least one piece of featured content, and the preview picture translates and formats correctly.

☐ I have written at least one article using LinkedIn's native blog publisher and added it to my "Featured Content" section.

☐ My "About" section shows readers who I am, in the first person, with no fluff words.

☐ My "Experience" section is filled out, up-to-date, accurate, data-centric, and includes supporting media for visual completion.

☐ My education, licensure, certifications, and volunteer experience are entered correctly.

☐ I have entered all available skills keywords.

☐ I have endorsed a colleague's skills and requested reciprocity.

☐ I have thoroughly filled in my volunteer activities.

☐ I have written at least five recommendations for colleagues and requested they each write one in return.

☐ My profile has been reviewed by a trusted colleague for overall impression, typos, and grammar.

Still feeling overwhelmed? Want to see me build a completely optimized LinkedIn profile from scratch?

Well, you're in luck! I break it all down step-by-step in this video:

https://linkedinprofile.adambraatz.com

CHAPTER 7

Building A Powerful LinkedIn Network

I don't know why I did it, but I did.

A fellow veteran, a 2nd-degree connection, had replied to an original post of mine in a way that had really irked me. His intent was entirely harmless, but I still chided him. I was incredibly rude to this dude for no good reason. It's one thing to kick the beehive a bit, but I admit that my behavior was simply uncalled for and said much more about me than it did about him.

Then he did something absolutely incredible in response. He was nice to me. When I say "nice," I mean NICE. He initiated a connection and sent me a direct message which was kind and conciliatory. Ashamed, I apologized, and he quickly shrugged it off. He was already over it. This guy, clearly a much bigger man than I, absolutely killed me with kindness. I learned a valuable and enduring lesson in that exchange.

Once again, I was reminded of how important it is to view digital engagement through a human lens. It's so easy to be unkind or dismiss someone's feelings in a digital landscape, but that doesn't make it right. As I mentioned before, we're often rude online to folks that we would otherwise have been perfectly pleasant to in person.

As you build your LinkedIn network, you'll come across all types of people who bring with them a variety of experiences and backgrounds. I believe that with the right mindset it's possible to flip the script. What if we were kind to people online who we would typically avoid or potentially quarrel with if we were face-to-face? We may not be able to change the way everyone behaves online, but I firmly believe that we can make a positive impact by leading the way.

To this day, the gentleman from this exchange checks in with me occasionally with his trademark kindness and upbeat attitude. He's one of my favorite people on LinkedIn.

It can be tempting to forgo the niceties and build your network as quickly as possible, but we must remember that just because someone is following you on a social platform does not mean you have a relationship with them. It doesn't mean your connection is real or valuable. There are inadvisable shortcuts out there that will make your network grow to a massive size almost overnight. Not only are they complete wastes of time and money, they could easily damage your real network prospects. Resist the urge to rush through the process of developing your network. Instead, remain focused on the long game of relationship-building. Plant seeds, water and care for them, and patiently wait for them to flourish. If you jump the gun, your harvest will not reach its full potential.

There are no legitimate shortcuts. There are no hacks, no cheats, no quick fixes. Think about how you developed friendships throughout school. Were you able to force those connections? How many of them were superficial? How much time and genuine effort did the development of true friendships take? Those relationships grew organically, slow and steady. As with your early friendships, being yourself is the way to go on LinkedIn too. Fake and manipulative behaviors may garner you superficial gains in the short term, but they rarely yield lasting or mutually beneficial results. Being genuine and authentic, even when it's difficult, is the key to enduring growth. If anyone has a problem with the real you, they aren't really worth your time anyway. Read that last sentence again. Maybe twice.

When I get to this part of a consultation with a client, I'm frequently asked how often I advise someone to check in and interact with their network on LinkedIn. Here's what I often hear. "I'm already on three different social networks! I can't even wrap my brain around adding another one! It's just too much!"

I can sympathize. But there's a serious disconnect with that mindset. As is the case with most things in your professional and personal life, the more time you put into something, the more benefit you will see. Creating a LinkedIn profile and allowing it to grow mold while you sit around and wait to reap the benefits makes zero sense. Has that approach ever worked for you? Would you buy an exercise bike and expect the pounds to melt away without climbing on the thing? If you devote more dedicated effort to curating and stewarding your professional network on LinkedIn, it will likely grow and lead you to opportunities. If you don't, it likely won't.

Some people are capable of diving into a new endeavor headfirst and need to be reminded that slow and steady wins the race. Others desire to ease into things or are hesitant to embark upon new endeavors. Take your time if you need to. Slow down if you have to. This is a highly personal journey. Whatever frequency of checking in on the platform is right for you, just be consistent with it. I would, at an absolute bare minimum, access LinkedIn once a day to check your notifications, direct messages, and interact with your network a bit.

As your network grows, I want you to consider the importance of connection points. *Connection points are the commonalities you and others share that can be leveraged to initiate a connection.* They're fantastic icebreakers for potential new LinkedIn pals. Every time a connection point is established, a window of opportunity opens. These include, but are not limited to, if you:

- ✸ both served in the military, in the same branch, or in the same area of responsibility
- ✸ went to the same university
- ✸ worked in the same career field, industry, or for the same company
- ✸ reside in the same general area
- ✸ have a friend or family member that may have served in the same organization or military unit
- ✸ commented on the same post and seem to share an opinion or perspective on the original topic
- ✸ had any kind of positive back-and-forth on LinkedIn

In addition to having your radar up for possible connection points with potential network connections, you should also consider the connection points you're broadcasting to the wider LinkedIn world. During the previous section, I suggested that using a city skyline for the banner photo on your profile may be an effective option because a potential connection visiting your profile may see your banner and think, *Hey, I've been there!* Or subconsciously feel connected to you because of your shared residency. That's a perfect example of establishing a potential connection point.

YOUR FIRST 500 CONNECTIONS

Under your headline in your profile intro section, LinkedIn publicly displays how many total connections you have. If you have 500 or more connections, that number will read as 500+. It doesn't matter if you have 501 or the LinkedIn maximum of 30,000, it will still display as 500+. Accordingly, many folks aspire to earn their 500+ stripes as quickly as possible. As I stated earlier, moving slowly and deliberately with your digital network development is the ideal long-term approach. LinkedIn agrees with me. They want all their users to have a logical reason for requesting a connection with someone new. Haphazardly connecting with random people without a deliberate thought process doesn't bring value to either party.

Though LinkedIn evangelizes this approach, they also infuriatingly sit on both sides of the fence. They openly express a desire for you to personally know every single person that you request a connection with. At the same time, the platform has a "People You May Know" section in the network tab which allows you to rapid fire requests, Rambo-style. Yet they limit the number of outgoing requests you can send and will even scold or punish you for overdoing it. Quit sending us mixed signals, LinkedIn.

FROM LINKEDIN.COM:

We have invitation limits in place to protect our overall member experience and to ensure that our members only receive relevant requests. Your LinkedIn account may be temporarily restricted from sending invitations to people for the following reasons:

✸ *You've sent many invitations within a short amount of time.*

✸ *Many of your invitations have been ignored, left pending, or marked as spam by the recipients.*

Note: *To ensure an optimal site experience, the network size limit for LinkedIn members is a maximum of 30,000 1st-degree connections. We recommend that you only keep quality connections in your network. To ensure that LinkedIn remains a safe community, we recommend that you only send invitations to people you know and trust, in accordance with LinkedIn's User Agreement and Professional Community Policies.*

So the popular question is, "Should I know each and every connection personally?" If you ask fifty different LinkedIn users for advice on this topic, you'll likely get a handful of different answers. Ironically, some of the influencers who would respond with an emphatic "yes" have hit their 30,000-connection maximum. That's a lot of people. I seriously doubt most people with that many connections could successfully pick 29,500 of them out of a lineup. Sure, influencers on LinkedIn can be inspiring, motivational, and educational. But their disingenuousness can still be overwhelmingly palpable. Always question your sources when it comes to advice on LinkedIn best practices.

Here's my opinion. Should you know each LinkedIn connection personally? No. Give me a break. Should you have some semblance of a connection point or a potential connection point with each of them? Yes.

Start your LinkedIn network growth journey by sending connection requests to your family, friends, past and current coworkers, and people with whom you've served. Those are the most obvious and logical connection points. Most people I coach are surprised with how many connections this first step yields. Heck, it can hit the hundreds. And follow a few businesses, brands, or influencers for good measure.

Many veterans find it comfortable to network almost exclusively with their military brothers and sisters, in person and online. It's a great place to start, but take deliberate steps to venture outside of the military bubble. You'll find it challenging to grow professionally in the civilian work world if you avoid networking with civilians. Lean on your veteran fraternity, but then branch out. More on that later.

YOUR NETWORK, BY THE NUMBERS

The following are three of the most common questions I receive about LinkedIn network growth and my answers:

How many outgoing connection requests can you send?

I'm convinced that nobody outside of LinkedIn actually knows the real answer to this question. Many argue that the number is dependent upon your level of activity on the platform. Outgoing invitations for events and requests to follow company pages also count toward your outgoing request total. LinkedIn will typically warn you when you're getting a bit too heavy-handed with the outgoing requests—typically around 80-100 a day. If you get the warning, stop. Otherwise you risk being punished by having features disabled for hours, days, or longer. "LinkedIn jail" is never fun.

Where can I see my pending and outgoing connection requests and invitations?

Click on the "My Network" tab on either desktop or mobile. On desktop, click "Manage" on the right side on the top of the main content section, then "Sent." On mobile, touch "Invitations," then "Sent." Regardless of how many requests you send per day, if you have too many outgoing requests in the queue, it's rumored that LinkedIn will throttle back your content reach. I frequently check my outgoing invitations to ensure there aren't too many piled up. Depending upon how ravenously you want to go after network expansion, it's easy to rack up hundreds of outgoing requests. If you have a large amount to clear out, I find it more efficient to do so via the mobile app.

What if someone doesn't respond to my request?

It's fairly common for LinkedIn users to check in on their LinkedIn accounts less frequently than, say, Facebook. Don't be offended if it takes a few weeks for your target to see and respond to your connection request. That said, if an outgoing connection request hasn't been responded to after one month, I typically withdraw the request. Same goes for company page invitations.

SEARCHING THE DATABASE

LinkedIn is first and foremost a database. In fact, it's the world's largest professional database, and by leveraging its powerful search tools, users can grow their professional networks in a strategic and targeted fashion.

Basic (free) plan users have a limit on the number of searches they can do in a given period of time, which I've used up more than once. Especially when I was getting started. Don't forget to take advantage of the free Premium deal LinkedIn offers to service members and veterans, as that will afford you a greater number of searches. The actual number of searches they allow for basic and premium users is closely guarded and rumored, again, to be dependent upon your overall individual usage of the platform. That said, I've never hit a limit on searches while a Premium user, so I assume the number is rather high.

USING SEARCH FEATURES EFFECTIVELY

Hopefully, you're still contemplating growing your professional network on LinkedIn with connection points in mind. You'll be doubling down on those connection points in due course. Follow this simple, step-by-step process to get started:

⊛ Put your cursor into the search bar and press "Enter" on desktop or "Search" on mobile without entering any text.

⊛ Click on "People," then click the "Connections" drop-down and hit "2nd" and "3rd+." If you already have a relatively developed network, you don't have to select "3rd+."

⊛ Click "Location" and search for the region where you are looking for a job. This could be your current residential area, where you hope to reside after transitioning from the military, or both.

⊛ Hit "All Filters" and whittle down your search results using relevant connection points. Start by leveraging your military family. Let's say you're retiring from the Navy, moving to San Antonio, and aspire to work as an engineer. Refine your search to the greater San Antonio Area, then search for professionals who have "United States Navy" as a past company. Add your industry. Continue to chip away until you have between 50-250 search results. If you can find 50 or more Navy veteran engineers who live and work around San Antonio, you've struck gold. If you can't find that many, zoom out your focus a bit by taking away search filter criteria.

⊛ Send connection requests to these people with a personalized invitation message. I'll talk about best practices below.

HEADS UP!

LinkedIn Premium users are able to see everyone who has clicked on and viewed their profile, which can be a valuable tool to use as you grow your professional network.

It also works both ways.

This means that if your target is a Premium user and you click on his/her profile, they may know that you were taking a look. Viewing people's profiles isn't something to be self-conscious about for the most part. Just think twice before you check up on your old boss or ex-girlfriend/boyfriend.

CHECK IT OUT!

See how I use LinkedIn's search features to find potentially fruitful connections with the right kind of people in this video:

 https://linkedinsearch.adambraatz.com

CHAPTER 8

Stewarding Your New Relationships

REACHING OUT TO YOUR NETWORK

It can be awkward to reach out to someone new for the first time. Follow these rules to ensure you don't make a LinkedIn connection request faux pas:

- ✸ Make sure there's a logical point of connection or, ideally, multiple points of connection between you and your potential new acquaintance.

- ✸ Always send a personalized message with your connection request. On desktop, you'll be asked if you want to send a note along with your connection request. On mobile, you must go to your target's full profile, touch the three dots icon, then select "Personalize Invite." Do this *every time*. The formula for a great personalized invite is as follows:

  - Hi/hello (first name).

  - Mention your mutual connection points. Namedrop where appropriate.

  - Say why you desire to connect.

  - End with "I would be honored if you would join my LinkedIn network" or something similar.

Put together, the above formula looks something like this:

"Hi John, always happy to connect with a fellow Marine! I'm actually retiring and moving to your neck of the woods in October. I'd be honored if you would join my LinkedIn network."

- Your invitation to connect should never, under any circumstances, be phrased in a way that could even remotely be interpreted as a request for a favor. Not for help finding a job, not for connections, not to look at your résumé. Nothing. Do not ask for anything. This is not the time nor place.

- There's a good chance a fellow vet from your branch who resides in your area—who may even be in the same industry or know some of the same people—will offer to connect with you in person or help out. Let them make that move. And if and when it happens, graciously accept.

- Do *not* attach anything to this personalized note, especially not your résumé. This can be a huge turn off for your potential connections. If they specifically ask for something, by all means, feel free to send it along.

- Do *not* ask to meet in person. Not in this first message at least.

- Do *not* ask them to "hop on a call" or send them a link to register for a Zoom meeting. Only poorly trained salespeople do this.

- Do *not* say anything about a business opportunity you have in mind for them.

- *Do* connect simply for the sake of connecting. You're planting seeds here, not harvesting.

- Namedropping is an acceptable practice if leveraged in the right way. After all, you can see who your target is connected with before sending your connection request. Only namedrop if the person you're naming is aware that you're doing so or knows you well enough that they won't draw a blank if your name comes up. If you namedrop and your target reaches out to that person to verify and they reply with something like, "I have no idea who that is," then your new relationship is dead in the water. Especially if you're namedropping a mutual military connection.

  Here's an example:

  "I see you're connected with Jack Jackinson too. I served with him at the 737TRG! Small world."

- If you've already transitioned out of the military, even if it was years ago, you still have a several-year lease on the "new guy/new gal" badge. You can say you're still transitioning or are new to an area with a couple of years under your belt.

- Military shorthand is just fine in a direct message, but only if the recipient likely has knowledge of what you're referring to.

INMAIL – WHAT, WHEN, AND WHERE?

I have a confession to make. I'm pretty sure I've only sent a few InMails in my life, and most of those occasions were by accident when I was just getting started. I can attest to the fact that you definitely do not need to send InMails to grow a powerful network on LinkedIn. That said, studies show that InMails have an even higher open and response rate

---

65

than regular emails that contain the same content. Your LinkedIn Premium account lets you send up to five InMails per month. Any leftover credits roll over for up to three months.

Several connections I respect quite a bit have told me they use InMails to initiate a conversation with someone they really want to add to their network, like a whale of a prospect, a well-known influencer, or a business leader. Play around with it. You may find they're super useful for you. Let me know if you do.

HEADS UP!

It's shocking how frequently strangers on LinkedIn will ask you to "hop on a call" to "get to know you" or "learn more about your business". I'd say 98% of the time, they're merely trying to sell you something or get you to unwittingly become part of a sales funnel.

Unfortunately, these tactics do work on some people, and veterans are a common target. If they didn't work from time to time, the practice wouldn't be so common.

It's an incredibly shortsighted approach, though, and I wouldn't recommend it. So what should you do if you get a request like this? It's your call at the end of the day but consider the following:

- *Do you know and trust this person? Have you interacted in any way? Why would they want to connect with you?*

- *Would it be worth your time? Remember, nobody is entitled to your time and attention, and there is absolutely nothing wrong with asking clarifying questions to make an informed decision.*

If the answers to any of these questions is no, politely decline. Or if the only interaction you've had with them is the request to "hop on a call," it's fine to just ignore them and move on with your life.

A young professional from my local area reached out to me via LinkedIn. He seemed to be a go-getter with a polished profile and some compelling content. I accepted his connection request, and we started to chat via direct message. I don't always chat like that with a new connection. In fact, I typically avoid it. But he initiated a dialogue, so I politely responded. This was early in my LinkedIn journey when I didn't know any better.

I was in high-volume-networking mode, so I was trying to cast as wide a net as possible with my professional networking. When he asked to connect in person, I agreed without hesitation, and we set a time for coffee. We met, sat down, and had an enjoyable conversation about our jobs, aspirations, and families. My thought? Hey, this guy could become a good friend!

Cue the sound of a record scratch. It was as if someone had flipped a switch. He looked into my eyes and said, "Should we get started?" then pulled out his binder and proceeded to launch unabashedly into a full-scale pitch for his financial management and insurance services.

The first part of our meeting was so nice, and the pitch portion was so cringeworthy that I found myself personally affronted by the whole thing. I couldn't get a word in. He gave me his ENTIRE pitch. I finally told him, "Sorry man, I'm just not a good customer for you. My wife and I have a financial adviser, so we're covered there."

To which he mumbled a few sentences, got awkward, stood up, and said he had another meeting to get to. He slunk away and left me with the bill for our fancy lattes. It was such a disappointing encounter that I sent him an email later that day telling him as much.

He responded defensively, then disconnected with me on LinkedIn.

Had the guy from the story skipped the pitch and just hung out, I'm sure we would've connected again. We legitimately could've been friends. Imagine how many quality prospects I might've sent his way! If my wife and I had suddenly needed a new adviser, reaching out to him would've been a no-brainer. He could've potentially gotten so much business from me by being a friend instead of a salesperson — without making a single pitch. This young man put all of his eggs in the short-term gain basket and undoubtedly failed to realize the long-term opportunity he missed. I doubt I was the only one he did this to. In his defense, I don't blame him at all. I blame poor training. I hope he figured it out.

Your professional network cultivation and stewardship is best kept almost entirely in the long-term gain basket. As I mentioned earlier, you simply can't rush this part. Network development, online or in person, is a lot like investing. If you need long-term monetary gains that you can cash in years or decades down the road, investing can get you there. If you need to get some scratch to pay the electric bill this Friday, starting a Roth IRA today will not be very helpful.

Traditional, old-school network development best practices suggest that you get in touch regularly with your connections. These frequent "touch points" keep you front of mind and help develop your relationship. Though that's still accurate, the landscape has changed so much that it seems like laughably anachronistic advice. This is due to the fact that touch points can now occur in ways that the originators of that approach never even dreamed of. Having a connection view your live-streamed business card unboxing while riding their Peloton absolutely counts as a touch point these days. Imagine going back in time and saying the previous sentences to a 1980's business visionary. I wonder what their reaction would be.

Folks, there are many ways to get in touch and even more avenues to stay in touch. This may be a stretch for some of you, especially the men. Generally speaking, men aren't as adept as women at keeping in touch with their friends and family. I'm an anomaly in that regard, but I recognize that most dudes don't operate that way. Regardless of your gender, adding some simple procedures to your thought process can help you along this path.

 HYBRID CONSIDERATIONS

Whenever I see a network connection of mine featured or mentioned in a publication of any kind, especially a traditional print publication, I snag a picture of it on my smartphone and send it to them in a direct message.

A quick message like, "Hey, I know a celebrity! Hope you are well!" or "You're famous! Congrats on the recognition" works great to reengage while also making your connection feel important.

Have you ever had an old friend pop into your head and thought, *Dang, I wonder what they're up to?* It's easier than ever to hunt those people down and send them a message, but inexplicably, many of us still don't take the time to reach out. Get in the habit of shooting off a quick message when you think of someone or when you see their content in your feed. You don't need a reason. In fact, it's better if you don't have a business goal in mind. It's perfectly acceptable to say, "Just checking in. Hope you're well!"

If you happen across a connection's content in your newsfeed, engage with it. This will give their content a boost and validate their efforts and insights. Engaging makes people feel appreciated and important. Leave a substantive comment on their post. Not "I agree" or something equally useless. If a post was especially impactful to you, don't be afraid to send the author a direct message telling them that. Again, don't ask for anything or make any pitches. I've found the comments sections of an original post to be one of the most reliable springboards to connect with new people and build relationships with my existing connections. Don't miss these valuable windows of opportunity.

You don't need to type out a lengthy message when you reconnect with your existing network. Keep it short and sweet. For the busy and overwhelmed—aren't we all?—LinkedIn's mobile app even allows you to record and send an audio message. This approach is also the least common way people reach out, which means it can really stand out. I was absolutely giddy to receive an audio reply message from the one and only Brendan Kane of *One Million Followers* and *Hook Point* acclaim. It was a really exciting experience and solidified my lifetime Brendan fandom.

Even more effective than interacting in comment sections and reaching out via direct message is acting as a connector, when appropriate. Instead of looking out for your own needs, job prospects, sales, or the like, focus on the needs of your connections. Do you know people who could solve someone else's problems or make their lives easier? Introduce them in a group direct message, explain why you're connecting them, rinse, and repeat. For example, is one of your connections expressing frustration with their marketing efforts? Connect them with a marketing whiz you know. It's that simple! More on that later.

YOUR SOCIAL SELLING INDEX

LinkedIn offers a proprietary tool called the Social Selling Index (SSI) that measures how effectively you're engaging with your network. This measurement is based on how frequently and effectively you establish your brand, find and connect with logical connections, create and engage with content, and build relationships.

LinkedIn boasts that paid program users typically have a significantly higher SSI due to their unencumbered access to LinkedIn's many features. Though I absolutely believe this to be true, please bear in mind that the SSI is used primarily as a means to encourage free users to upgrade. That said, it's always worth taking a look at.

CHECK IT OUT!

For an explanation of how LinkedIn scores its Social Selling Index and to view your personal SSI:

 **https://business.linkedin.com/sales-solutions/
social-selling/the-social-selling-index-ssi**

CULTIVATING CONNECTIONS

FROM LINKEDIN.COM:

"Your LinkedIn feed is made up of the conversations happening across your professional communities: among connections; in the groups you've joined; and the people, pages, and hashtags that you follow. To decide what goes at the top, we use look [sic] at who's talking (People You Know) and what they're talking about (Things You Care About). We're constantly working on improving and evolving the feed experience."

Sounds great, right? Unfortunately, the reality is your newsfeed is a wild beast that must be tamed and cared for. If neglected, it can get totally out of hand, bombard you with things that are irrelevant to you, make you angry, or try to sell you things you don't need or want.

LinkedIn will also send you content from users you engage more frequently or for longer durations of time. If you comment on someone's post, you'll likely be shown more content similar to it or from the same creator in the future. If you chat with a connection via direct messages, you'll be more likely to see their content in your feed as well. LinkedIn will also present you with more content from 2nd-degree connections that your 1st-degree connections engage with. Sometimes LinkedIn straight-up guesses what you would be interested in based on the mutual interests of your 1st-degree connections. Often, they get it right with haunting accuracy. Other times, they'll whiff completely. It is only a computer, after all, that's making calculations based on the information it's presented within the confines of the algorithm it's programmed to execute.

I strongly encourage you to view your newsfeed as a safe space, Zen space, or whatever you want to call it. There's no reason why anything in your newsfeed should bring negativity of any kind into your life. You can and should curate your newsfeed in a way that increases the quality and relevance of the content presented to you. The more relevant content, the more engagement opportunities you have.

As I tell anyone who complains about LinkedIn tossing them irrelevant garbage in their newsfeeds, "You have near-complete control of the quality of your feed at all times." First, you can decide whether or not you wish to prioritize content picked by LinkedIn or view posts in the order in which they're posted. Some folks prefer chronological. But even as wonky as LinkedIn's suggestions can be from time to time, I still prefer a curated feed. I would hate to miss out on a great post from a peer just because they posted from a different time zone. In the upper right corner of your feed, select "Top" for LinkedIn's curated feed or "Recent" for chronological presentation. Choose wisely. It can be hard to find, so here's a handy screen capture.

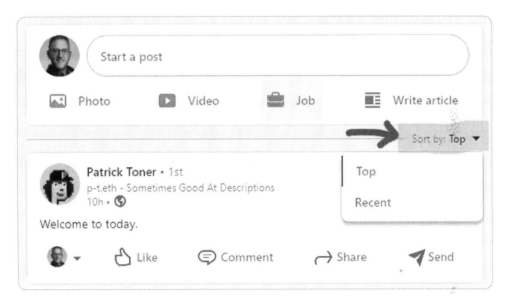

Whenever something shows up in your feed that you don't want to see, go on the offensive. By clicking the three dots in the upper right corner above each individual post, you'll see a selection of options that will give LinkedIn the information it needs to show you content more accurately that's compelling and relevant to you.

- ⊛ Unfollow: you'll stay connected with the person in question but will no longer see their content in your feed—the one I use most frequently.

- ⊛ Remove Connection: the LinkedIn equivalent of "unfriending."

- ⊛ Mute: use this to prevent content from folks who are not 1st-degree connections from showing in your feed.

- ⊛ I Don't Want To See This: tell LinkedIn why you aren't interested, and they'll stop showing you content similar to the post in question but won't necessarily mute the person doing the posting.

✴ Report Post: use this if the post is offensive, harmful, or if you suspect the account is fraudulent or hacked.

I use all of the above to curate my feed and leverage the "Unfollow" option with extreme prejudice. Again, our newsfeeds should be happy places. I don't need to see things that bring negativity into my life. The "Unfollow," "Remove Connection," and "Block" options are available by accessing any user's profile directly. Save blocking for extreme circumstances—garnering a reputation for blocking anyone who disagrees with you is a bad look—but don't hesitate to do so if someone is making you uncomfortable. After all, there are plenty of other business fish in the sea.

HEADS UP!

LinkedIn has recently revealed a feature that allows users to hide most political content from their newsfeeds. Go into "Settings," "Account Preferences," then look for the toggle under "Feed Preferences."

Feed preferences
Do you want to see political content in your feed?

Allow political content   Off

Learn more about how we define political content. Discover sources to follow.

On the flip side, everything you do on the platform has the chance of being presented to other users through LinkedIn's content curation algorithm—your posts, comments, follows, and even your likes. This is precisely why I generally avoid posting about or even engaging with polarizing or controversial topics like politics and religion. You know, the topics you would most likely fight with your drunk uncle about at Thanksgiving.

If your career is in politics or religion, well, live it up. In those circumstances, it would absolutely make sense to create and engage with that type of content. Otherwise, don't risk alienating your audience by delving off topic. For example, you may think that liking a politically charged post that you align with is harmless. But if it shows up in my feed that you did and I'm strongly philosophically opposed to the viewpoint, I may unfollow you. I don't need your "likes" dragging irrelevant content into my feed. It would be a shame if someone unfollowed you because of a political difference if they were otherwise a potentially awesome connection.

You can also give content that's valuable to you a "pat on the back" to help LinkedIn send more relevant stuff your way. If there's a connection or creator who frequently posts content you're fond of, head over to their profile and click the bell icon near the top. This will ensure that LinkedIn notifies you whenever that creator's content becomes available and also tell LinkedIn the type of person you're interested in hearing more from. No need to feel self-conscious about ringing the bell on your favorite LinkedIn pals' profiles—they won't be notified when you do. So don't be bashful. Head over to my profile and smash that bell icon.

CUTTING CORNERS

As I mentioned earlier, there are no shortcuts to effective network development. Not if you plan on having a network that generates reciprocal value. Sure, having 500+ connections may feel like a tiny badge of honor—and it is in many ways—but the number of connections or followers you have really and truly does not matter. Imagine someone bragging about a unit citation they're wearing when, in truth, they were on leave during the incident that earned it. It's all a show. All frosting, no cake.

I know a person who had two separate LinkedIn profiles, both of which had maxed out 1st-degree connections. That's a total of 60,000 connections between them. I vividly remember when he first told me about it. He proclaimed, bursting with pride, that his following was so large that he had to open up a second profile, which quickly maxed out. I rolled my eyes at this ludicrous proclamation so hard that I went blind for nearly twelve minutes. I don't think he really understood the difference between connections and followers.

The lightest scrutiny revealed the truth behind the numbers, and all it took was about three minutes of digging through his public profile. I started by looking at his activity, and sure enough, all of his original content had negligible engagement. Awfully strange for a profile with 30,000 "quality" professional connections! I suspected he'd bought followers or used a cheap automated program of some kind to build his network. I verified my hunch by using LinkedIn's search features on his network connections and discovered that over 95% of them were from outside of the country. Nothing wrong with residing on foreign soil, of course. I just seriously doubt he had mutually beneficial business relationships with over 29,500 professionals who lived in Auckland or Bangladesh. Chances are that a majority of these accounts were fake to begin with. Imagine wasting your time and money acquiring 60,000 toothless connections that had no impact whatsoever. No value or benefit to be found anywhere. Just an unjustifiably inflated ego. Sad stuff.

You can easily use this same tactic to vet your own LinkedIn connections, which I often do when a stranger tries to pitch their trashy automated LinkedIn growth services to me. It may sound harsh, but why would anyone pay for LinkedIn network growth services from someone with a completely worthless network themselves? I usually inform them, courteously, that their approach isn't the way.

Yes, it is possible to buy and acquire mass followers through a variety of unsavory means, all of which are as unadvisable as the next. Don't do it. Just don't. I promise you'll receive and provide no value, and you'll regret going down that path. Many realize the error of their ways after the fact, but the damage done by acquiring 30,000 mostly fake connections is nearly irreversible. I have unfortunately advised a handful of folks in this situation to start a new profile from scratch. Take your lumps, learn, and move on.

HYBRID CONSIDERATIONS

Whenever I travel for work, I usually take a minute to search through my network connections in the area where I'm headed. I have, on several occasions, met face to face with LinkedIn connections while on the road for no reason other than to put a face to the name.

Don't be shy about doing this, especially with fellow veterans. Remember, your in-person and digital networking endeavors are exceptionally powerful when combined.

Additionally, if you post original content and engage with your LinkedIn network frequently, don't be surprised if you run into people who recognize you, especially at business-related events, conferences, or conventions.

I'm not a well-known LinkedIn influencer by any means, but I have heard, "Hey I know you from LinkedIn!" more times than you would probably believe. The first time it happened, I was thoroughly disarmed and reacted with superlative awkwardness.

HEADS UP!

If you take my hybrid networking advice above, it is advisable to take some precautions. Chances are slim, but you never know if the other person is dangerous. After all, there are crazies everywhere, and they seem to love hanging out on the internet.

My advice is to use the same strategy you would employ for a blind date: meet in a public place and let someone know where you are going to be in advance.

Please, be safe.

CHAPTER 9

Content Creation for LinkedIn

"Just start."

That's what my friend Quentin "Q" Allums told me, and I daresay he knows what he's talking about. After all, he is a globally-known influencer, TEDx speaker, podcaster, and widely recognized as one of the quintessential pioneers of video content on LinkedIn.

"Just start" turned out to be some of the best advice I've ever received.

Luckily at the time, Q resided just down the road from where I worked and graciously agreed to a sit-down. In a coffee shop, on a lovely spring morning in downtown Milwaukee, he patiently allowed me to pick his brain about professional growth through LinkedIn. I had become more active there in the beginning of that year but felt compelled to do more. I saw immense potential in the platform. But I needed some guidance on how to move forward. In the span of about fifteen minutes, the guy dropped about a hundred monumentally profound insights and truth bombs on me.

The conversation went something like this:

Me: I want to do a 30-day LinkedIn video challenge.

Which meant committing to post a video a day for at least 30 days.

Q: Why?

Me: No idea. It's just something I want to do. I feel like I have things to say and want to expand my network.

Q: Cool. Do it.

Me: When should I start? What are the best days/times to post?

Q: Right now.

Me: I want to make sure I'm doing it right.

Q: Don't worry about that. Just do it.

Me: Well, I've got some planning and work to do before I launch.

Q: No, you don't, man. Just start. And keep going. And don't worry about reach, or algorithms, or anything like that.

Me: Really? It's that simple?

Q: It's not easy, but yes, it is that simple.

He told me to take my phone out, record video #1, and announce that I was doing a 30-day video challenge.

I did.

Then he encouraged me to post it to LinkedIn, right then and there.

I did.

And boom! Instant public accountability.

Around the same time, the infinitely wise guru of marketing Judi Murphy shared that the key to brand development, personal or otherwise, is consistency over time. Q was essentially saying the same thing, with the added caveat to not stress about it. They were—and still are—both right.

Since I completed the 30-day challenge all those years ago, my network has exploded with meaningful connections. Through content creation, I've been fortunate to garner career advancements, had countless business and entrepreneurial opportunities, been invited to be a guest on a handful of podcasts, and developed professional connections that will last a lifetime. Even better, I've been able to leverage my network to help others in their networks, careers, and professional development.

None of that happened because my videos had epic organic reach or thousands of views. A good handful of the videos were a complete flop by that metric. I wish I could say I had a steady, gradual increase in reach and *engagement throughout the process. Truth be told, there seemed to be no rhyme or reason to it at all. I had no idea if what I was doing was "right," if I was posting at the most advantageous times, or if my content was any good. I often wondered if I was wasting my time.*

But I stuck with it, following Q and Judi's advice. I posted consistently and made interacting with people a priority. I also prioritized being a giver and a connector.

I can't guarantee 100% that posting content on a regular basis and engaging with people in a positive fashion will explode your network and influence on this platform. But if you're vigilant, consistent, and don't waste time doubting yourself, I do like your chances.

HOW TO CREATE A POWERFUL LINKEDIN PRESENCE

People, especially fellow veterans, tend to hem and haw when I inform them that they should be creating and sharing original content on LinkedIn as often as is feasible. "Do I have to?" is the typical refrain. Some of these people post on Facebook, Instagram, and Twitter fourteen times a day, but somehow LinkedIn is a problem for them. Sharing your thoughts on a platform which could actually lead to some benefit for all parties involved is too much for you to handle? I just don't get it.

If you want to grow your network into an absolute powerhouse and begin leveraging it for the benefit of all mankind as quickly as possible, then yes, you need to create some stinking content, for cryin' in the mud—said with my thickest-possible Wisconsin accent. If you didn't skip any of the sections leading up to this one, you'll know exactly why by now. If you did skip, go back and read. Puh-lease.

Now that we're talking about the content itself, there are some added benefits we haven't touched on yet. Here are a few great reasons why you need to be an active contributor on LinkedIn:

❋ It allows you to establish yourself as a subject-matter expert, savvy social commentator, inspirational thinker, or all of the above. Being a trusted voice is one of the most insanely effective business and career multipliers.

❋ It can facilitate an exponential, snowball effect on your network growth.

❋ Many find that posting on LinkedIn frequently improves their copywriting skills. Imagine having more effective correspondences through your emails, text messages, or Slack channels.

❋ Each time your network sees or engages with your content, it counts as a touch point. As your reach expands, you'll be able to hit more and more birds with the same stone. It's nearly impossible to grow your LinkedIn network in a way that will have a meaningful impact on your career or business prospects without some semblance of content creation—that is, unless you're already monumentally famous. I'm sure if

Stephen Spielberg decided to hop on LinkedIn, he would have a hundred thousand engaged followers overnight. But for us mere mortals, expecting to achieve next-level results while living out your days as a LinkedIn hermit is straight-up foolishness.

THE FABLED ALGORITHM

In the previous section, we touched on LinkedIn's algorithm—the expansive formula that decides what content is seen by whom, when, and at what frequency. Every social network has a content algorithm, which they all guard very closely. Few professionals outside of these organizations truly know the ins and outs of their respective social algorithms. If made public, "growth hackers" could exploit the algorithm for cheap views and followers. Over time, however, folks are able to deduce what resonates and what doesn't through trial and error. In my humble opinion, it's better that way.

You may hear content creators boasting about how they tricked, hacked, or "gamed" the LinkedIn algorithm. Ignore them and their advice. Unless they're former LinkedIn employees who worked directly with the content algorithm and are feeling brave enough to violate a nondisclosure agreement, their advice is anecdotal at best. These tactics are known in the social media and search-engine-optimization (SEO) world as "black hat" tactics and aren't worth your time. Besides, if anyone is actually able to "trick" the algorithm to help their content get more reach, every social platform is fairly adept at sniffing it out and making the necessary changes to close the loophole. Your trickery would be rendered instantaneously useless and also make you susceptible to being banned from the platform. I've seen it happen.

When it comes to getting started with content creation, you only need a cursory understanding of how an algorithm works. Don't try to "game the algorithm." Focus instead on creating compelling, authentic content and fostering meaningful professional relationships. The long-term benefits of "white hat" tactics—centered around sustainable best practices and high quality, consistent content creation—far outweigh any short-term, superficial benefits you could grab from the alternative.

HOW LINKEDIN'S ALGORITHM WORKS (KIND OF)

When you post original content, there are a series of algorithmic filters which determine how visible that content will be. The first round of filters determines the initial quality of your post and sifts out unnecessary spam. If your post is obviously spam or predatory content of any kind, LinkedIn may immediately flag it and give you a slap on the wrist. This discipline could include having the post removed, having functionality of the platform restricted, or being flat-out banned for a period of time or forever. If your post clears this first round, it's presented to a small sampling of your audience.

This first sampling period is exceptionally important for the ongoing longevity of your post. Likes, comments, and shares accumulated in the first sixty minutes following your post add points that determine whether or not your content is shown to more people in your network. Dwell time—the amount of time a user spends reading or interacting with your post—also weighs heavily on the algorithm's determination.

Dwell time was added to LinkedIn's metrics in 2020 and is an important consideration for anyone hoping to engage their network with original content.

FROM LINKEDIN.COM:

"At a high level, each update viewed on the feed generates two types of dwell time. First, there is dwell time 'on the feed,' which starts measuring when at least half of a feed update is visible as a member scrolls through their feed. Second, there is dwell time 'after the click,' which is the time spent on content after clicking on an update in the feed."

If your network unfollows you or hides your content from their feed as a result of the post, it will greatly hinder the efficacy of your post. If your connections report your content as spam or flag it as offensive or in violation of the community guidelines, it's likely dead in the water. When these things happen, they're also likely to hurt the reach of your future posts as well. Remember, using these features to curate your own personal newsfeed is a must, but the practice goes both ways. All it takes is one incredibly unwise, polarizing, or offensive post to do some real long-term damage to your LinkedIn prospects.

Bear in mind that this is an exceptionally reductive view of an extremely complicated and deep-rooted mechanism. The algorithm is also frequently changed and updated. The best and only way to stay on top of things is to create compelling, genuine, consistent quality content, engage in an authentic fashion, and dedicate yourself to helping others. That is how you can "beat" the algorithm.

CHAPTER 10

Important Posting Considerations (Q&A)

Below are samples of the questions I most frequently receive from veteran and military spouse clients about posting original content.

How often should I post?

The answer is different for everyone. Post at whatever frequency you can maintain. Consistency is significantly more important than volume. Be consistent, consistently. If posting two times a week is all you have the bandwidth for, then post two times a week. If you can realistically post once a day, even better. Posting once a week for a short period—only to disappear for a few weeks when you run out of ideas or when life gets busy—is not advisable. Some find it advantageous to ease their way into it.

When should I post?

The answer varies from network to network. My network may be active on LinkedIn, and thus more likely to view and engage with my content at different times than your network. Certain subject areas may get more traction with a portion of my network in the morning, while the evening crowd may be looking for something entirely different. It will take trial and error to figure what kind of content resonates with your particular audience(s) and when.

You didn't answer my question. When should I post?

Start with Tuesday and Thursday mornings between 7:00-9:00 a.m. CST and go from there. On Monday mornings, working professionals are typically focused on starting their week and catching up on emails from the previous week and weekend. On Fridays, folks are already dreaming about the weekend. In my experience, my content absolutely dies on Fridays. I've also had good luck with Saturday posts later in the morning or early afternoon. Other than that, trial and error is your friend. You may find that your network is absolutely ravenous for content related to manufacturing on Wednesday afternoons. The way your network responds to content and when is entirely unique and nuanced, and none of these suggestions are foolproof. In fact, I'm pretty sure I posted my most viral post on a Friday afternoon.

Someone is replying to my content with rudeness. What should I do?

Trolls are everywhere. LinkedIn is definitely no exception. When you're presented with trolling and negativity, you have five options in my humble estimation:

1. Kill them with kindness (as in the story from the previous section).

2. Kick the beehive.

If a 2nd or 3rd-degree connection hops into one of my posts with rudeness, I sometimes elect to poke at them a little bit. Never match their level of rudeness, anger, or vitriol. Or at least try not to. There's a delicate balance to strike, but when in doubt, a shrug or eyeroll emoji is usually more effective than a lengthy monologue. If they take the bait and reply further, it doesn't matter how they're feeling personally. Whether they agree with you or not, LinkedIn still views their additional replies as engagements, and your content will be pushed to more people as a result. You can then rally your network around you if you so desire. See below.

3. Rally your network around you.

You can rally your network to your aid without kicking the beehive, or you can take both approaches back-to-back. It's always preferable to have your network rush to your aid and defend you against the rudeness of folks trolling your content. If your connections rush to your defense by replying against negative comments without you reaching out, that signifies that your network is truly becoming powerful. Sometimes, you will need to reach out for support though. Try sending a direct message to a trusted colleague and ask for backup. If you find your network electing to not support you and the negative comments and replies start piling up, that can be an indicator that you may have misjudged the quality of your original post. When you reach out to your colleagues for backup, try asking if you're missing something or have blind spots. Your best friends are the ones who will let you know if you're out of line or have missed the mark. You also may have unintentionally—or heck, intentionally—said something offensive or unpopular.

4. Ignore them.

5. Block them and move on with your life.

Don't hesitate to take the latter two approaches if someone is being particularly nasty. Often, nastiness is disguised as someone "playing devil's advocate" or just "trying to have an honest debate." Though there are people out there who enjoy discourse with strangers online, I've found it to be incredibly rare for any of them to actually be in search of a good faith debate. Life is too short to abide negativity and trolling. You don't need people like that in your professional network.

What do I do if it turns out that my post was inadvisable or massively unpopular?

Weigh your options. Stand your ground, take your lumps, and face the consequences and long-term ramifications. Or delete the post and move on. I've done both. In either circumstance, you have a great opportunity for a follow-up post. Apologize for the insensitivity of your deleted post and vow to take an objective assessment or share the importance of sticking to your guns. Be warned, though, doubling down on a massively unpopular post could do some real damage.

What sort of things should I post about?

Go with what you know. Do you have any original thoughts or ideas? Of course you do! Do you have opinions about your industry, your workplace, your career field, or your professional discipline? Do you have successes or accomplishments to share? We'll talk more about how to get started in the next section, and you can check out the appendix for some content prompts if you're still stuck. A note of caution. Sometimes it's good to be careful about sharing your opinions.

What kind of mediums should I use to post?

There are a variety of ways to tell your story on LinkedIn: text posts, images with captions, videos, articles, or shared external links. LinkedIn even used to have a "Stories" feature like Facebook, Snapchat, or Instagram. You should try to use all of the above. A majority of my content is text-based, but I also post the occasional video, image, or external link. Mix it up and see what works. Rumor has it the algorithm rewards users who use more of LinkedIn's features.

What if I'm an introvert?

Believe it or not, I'm an introvert too. I'm what many call an extroverted introvert. I can be perfectly social, but it's exhausting. After conventions or conferences, I usually need to take a dang nap. But remember, just like lifting weights to beef up your muscles, discomfort fosters growth, and if you don't use it, you lose it. Take baby steps outside of your comfort zone and slowly work your way forward. You'll be surprised at what you are capable of.

Can I use colorful language?

You mean swearing? No. Would you swear in a job interview? If you want to use more "colorful language," do so sparingly. If you're currently seeking or anticipate seeking traditional employment at any time, I suggest avoiding it entirely.

But world-famous entrepreneur, author, and social media influencer Gary Vaynerchuk swears all the time!

Are you Gary Vaynerchuk?

No, I'm not Gary Vaynerchuk.

And . . . there you have it.

But, but, but . . .you tell people to be their true and authentic selves.

Correct, I definitely do. Are you honestly trying to tell me that you're incapable of being genuine or authentic without dropping f-bombs? If your entire identity and brand is based around that, then I suggest reevaluating. Being "edgy" isn't a whole personality. It sure isn't Gary Vee's.

What about politics, religion, or other potentially sensitive topics?

In case you missed it earlier, if you're a politician or aspiring politician, it would make sense to discuss politics on LinkedIn. If you're a religious leader, pastor, clergyman, or the like, then it's appropriate to discuss religious topics. Otherwise, I strongly suggest staying far away from it. Treat all other sensitive topics accordingly. Controversial or inflammatory content on LinkedIn can catch on like wildfire, but it isn't worth the risk of alienating whichever half of your network disagrees with your content. Imagine spending years to build your virtual consulting network, then having a single polarizing post go viral. Do you really want to be known for that? Are you willing—just to make a point—to have half of your audience unfollow you?

Should I avoid other people's political, religious, or otherwise controversial content?

Like the plague. Don't even like or comment on politically charged posts. The fact that you did may end up in someone else's news feed. Almost every day, I'm presented with "Jane Smith liked a post" in my newsfeed, only to discover that they "liked" a post that was distasteful or had a strong misalignment with my personal values. If the post they liked is unprofessional or doesn't jive with my values, I unfollow the perpetrator—and you should do the same. For the millionth time, newsfeed curation is an important part of your LinkedIn strategy and your overall social media mental health.

I have a crush on a connection or LinkedIn influencer. Should I hit them up?

No. LinkedIn is not a dating site. Don't be "that guy" or "that girl." Though women typically experience being hit on in their direct messages at a much higher rate than men, I've gotten it a few times myself. It's never, ever okay. I don't even reply. I just block them immediately. Though the military speaks a no-nonsense game when it comes to harassment of this kind, we all know that it often goes unpunished. The civilian world is less forgiving. As it should be. Your human resources department will terminate your employment without hesitation for a single inappropriate post, comment, or direct message—even if it's not directed at a fellow employee. If someone sees a vile comment and brings it to your civilian leadership's attention, you risk being canned. Some say that this qualifies as "cancel culture." I call it completely reasonable consequences for sexual harassment.

I see other people using LinkedIn in a way that I don't think fits with the professional atmosphere. Should I say something?

I wouldn't. I've seen these types of comments a hundred times:

- ✵ "Why would you post this on LinkedIn?"
- ✵ "This is a professional platform!"
- ✵ "This type of post doesn't belong on LinkedIn!"
- ✵ "Save it for Facebook!"

I call this "LinkedIn policing," and it's insanely annoying. It's also a 100% surefire way to get your beehive kicked by yours truly. Social networks are what they are—a living, evolving reflection of the people using them. As long as someone is interacting within LinkedIn's content guidelines, all other bets are off. If you think a post doesn't belong on LinkedIn because you have some altruistic idea of what you think the platform should be, just zip it and keep on scrolling. Engaging as the "LinkedIn Police" will only annoy other people and tell the algorithm that you'd like to see more content similar to the very content you're attempting to shut down.

What sort of posts should I avoid?

Aside from the aforementioned inflammatory or controversial topics, avoid content that would inspire eye rolls. Bragging is never cute, and users are adept at seeing right through a "humblebrag." Bragging disguised by a thin, disingenuous veil of humility. Do not copy others' content. Do not use the poll feature unless you're genuinely curious about the response and the question is relevant to what you're doing.

I work in banking/finance/insurance, and my content is strictly regulated. What can I do?

You have an uphill battle on your hands. Those who work in banking or under the umbrella of larger corporations have a mountain of compliance and regulation to contend with. Often, employees are only allowed to share preapproved content rather than generate something original. I can't wrap my brain around why any corporation thinks they have a right to control any employee's personal LinkedIn presence, but it is what it is. Sharing preapproved external links without even being allowed to add your two cents rarely gets any traction whatsoever. I'll explain how to get more out of sharing later in this section.

I'm drawing a blank. I don't know what to post. What should I do?

A content list is your best friend here. Use a cloud-based document program like Google Docs to keep an ongoing list of ideas. The handy thing about using cloud-based software is that you can open it up on your phone while you're out and about or on your desktop at home. If you're more old-school, keep a notebook in your pocket. Whenever an idea pops into your head, write it down. Then when you aren't quite sure what to post, reference your content document. Mine has saved me from writer's block more times than I can count.

Should I focus on quality, quantity, or both?

Ideally, both. The eventual goal is to produce a high volume of high quality posts. Getting to this point takes most people a fair amount of time, so focus on quality first and foremost. Never post garbage just because you need to meet a self-imposed frequency quota. As you grow and become more familiar with the platform and get more comfortable with the various kinds of content creation, you can work to increase the quantity or frequency.

Should I "like" my own posts?

There are two very different schools of thought on this topic. While I do typically like the content I produce, I do not click "like" on my own posts. I believe it comes off as desperate—not a good look at all. Others click "like" on every post and comment they make on their platform. I've heard advocates for this approach say, "Why would I share my content with the world if I don't like it? Why shouldn't I click 'like'?" I don't buy it, but hey, to each their own. I haven't seen enough of an algorithmic impact to justify being an own-post-liker.

HEADS UP!

Be deliberate about whatever you post. Assume that anything you put on the internet is inexorably eternal. Employers or future connections can and will see them. Opponents will try to leverage them against you.

Additionally, you never know when a post of yours will strike a chord and go viral. We don't get to choose when a post goes viral; all we can do is set it up for success. But weird things happen, and you'd hate for a post that does not truly represent you or your brand to absolutely blow up.

CHAPTER 11

Be Yourself
(Don't Be "That Person")

THE IMPORTANCE OF AUTHENTICITY

You should always start by posting about what you know and have personal experience with. Social media users, especially in younger demographics, can usually sniff out disingenuity from a mile away. Your target audience will not be fooled by claims of personal expertise with entirely anecdotal concepts or attempts to pass unoriginal content off as your own. But don't be discouraged. You have an entire lifetime's worth of experiences to draw from!

In my experience, the professional world truly resonates with content that's relatable, inspirational, aspirational, or a mix of all three. You can leverage one of these concepts or a combination of them in your online storytelling. Aspirational and inspirational content paint a picture of an achievable goal for your audience. Did you challenge yourself to lose twenty-five pounds before your daughter's wedding and succeed? Or did you fall short of the goal but learn a very important lesson?

Many military-type folks struggle with being vulnerable in a public setting, especially online for the whole world to see. Often, our community is guilty of viewing vulnerability as weakness and weakness tantamount with death. This couldn't be further from the truth. Within reason, vulnerability will not only make you relatable to your audience, it lends to your credibility. Notice that I said, "within reason." While vulnerability may inspire your audience, oversharing will inspire your audience to run for the hills.

You can make an aspirational or inspirational post out of just about anything. For example, let's say you got a flat tire on your way to work. Though the situation may be a pain in the butt, it presents you with an opportunity. You could snag a quick picture of your car sidelined on the highway and share how getting a flat tire taught you something about preparedness or risk management or whatever. Even more relatable and vulnerable, perhaps you could share about how your mechanic or spouse told you that your tires were bald and you needed new ones as soon as possible, but you didn't heed their advice in time and paid the price with a flat. Admitting that you were wrong and learned a valuable lesson is insanely relatable. Things that may seem mundane to you can be exceptionally interesting to your network when framed in an inspirational or aspirational way. These types of posts let people into your world and personality.

People love to help others, especially fellow veterans. Don't be afraid to ask for assistance in your public posts. This will give your network and potential network connections an opportunity to voluntarily share their expertise. Admit that you're new to all of this and ask for advice on various aspects of the platform. Ask for advice about military transition. Ask for advice about who to follow. Ask for résumé tips. Remember, you have a long, long lease on the "newbie" moniker, so don't hesitate to squeeze the maximum mileage out of it. People will either help out of the goodness of their hearts or because it makes them feel important to be helpful. Either way, this will put you on the community's radar and provide you with valuable opportunities to connect.

Posting about military experience is one of the most authentic things a service member or veteran can do, but we must approach this topic delicately. The general population supports you but doesn't always understand you. They'll put magnetic "support our troops" ribbons on their cars but avoid any kind of substantive dialogue about the real issues facing our community. To them, graphic details about combat are rarely relatable, aspirational, or inspirational. And often makes civilians uncomfortable. There's definitely a time and place for you to share those stories—and it's important that you do—but I'd be cautious about making it a staple of your LinkedIn content strategy.

An occasional story or anecdote about achieving something or overcoming a challenge related to your service, however, can really stand out if done correctly. Posts about you or a family member joining the military, completing training of some kind, receiving an award, or attaining a promotion are perfect. Same goes for posts that announce the conclusion of one's service when separating or retiring. Don't forget that the anniversary of each of the above occasions will make for a quality post as well.

LINKEDIN ARCHETYPES

There are numerous clichéd behaviors, personas, and patterns you'll see frequently while using this platform. Some of them can be really annoying and need to be taken seriously, as exhibiting or engaging with these behaviors can have a negative impact on your ability to grow your network. Additionally, if you have a battle buddy who is guilty of being "that guy" or "that gal," be a good friend and let them know. I would want someone to tell me.

Disclaimer: being your authentic self is the goal, and learning how to express your authentic self online is a long journey. Some people are further along on their LinkedIn brand development journey than others. The point of my "don't be that guy/gal" list is not judgment or condemnation. It's merely a cheeky exploration of silly behaviors many of us have been guilty of—me included. If you've been "that guy" at some point, don't beat yourself up. Learn from it and move on. For the most part, the following behaviors are problematic because they're phony or do not abide by the standard etiquette of the platform.

The Spray-and-Pray Résumé Launcher

This person posts their résumé anywhere and everywhere—on their profile, as original content, and in direct messages—often without context. This one happens so frequently within the military and veteran ecosystem that I wonder if it's part of the transition curriculum. I've been sent résumés by complete strangers without so much as a "hello" more times than I can count. Rule of thumb: do NOT send your résumé to anyone unless they ask for it. Also, your résumé should be tailored for each position you apply for, so posting one in your feed or on your profile rarely makes sense. Don't be that person.

The Let's-Hop-on-a-Call Person

As your network grows, you'll start to get connection requests that are accompanied by direct messages requesting that you "hop on a call" with the sender. These new connections often "just want to get to know more about you and your business." Unfortunately, 92% of the time, these folks are takers who want nothing more than to put you into a sales pipeline. A majority of messages like this are sent via automation software, which is a telltale sign that the person on the other end only cares about what they can get from you. If you receive messages like this, be skeptical. Also don't be that person.

The Exclusive-Business-Opportunity Bandit

Do you remember those scam emails from the crowned prince of a war-torn foreign country in the throes of civil war who just so happened to randomly select you to inherit his fortune before making his heroic escape? Well, this is the modern LinkedIn equivalent. I would argue that any stranger who offers you an exclusive, life-changing business opportunity out of the blue does not have your best interest at heart. Ask yourself, "Why would this stranger pick me out of all of the millions of available options out there?" If it doesn't make complete sense, that's a red flag. Don't be this person either.

The Vet Bro

Fairly often, I joke around about the stereotypical "vet bro" or "bro vet." I've heard it both ways. If you don't know the type of person I'm talking about, check out the video in the link below. There's no judgment here, and it's all in good fun. Heck, I check a lot of those boxes myself, and we should all be able to laugh at ourselves.

When it comes to LinkedIn content, there is something much less comical to consider than tactical vet bro attire. LinkedIn vet bros often act as if their military experience makes them an expert on all aspects of the military and foreign policy, especially compared to civilians. I have, unfortunately, seen countless vets get into fiery debates, act like condescending jerks, and unjustifiably claim firsthand expertise or knowledge on a topic. For example, I've been to Iraq but wouldn't dare to claim a superior understanding of Middle Eastern foreign policy as a result. Best practices for getting sand out of your boots, though? Yep, I'm your guy. Your military experience doesn't automatically make you more credible than civilians about all things military, and pretending that it does is never a good look. Potential connections and employers are watching, so don't be that person.

CHECK IT OUT!

We've all seen them. The Grunt-style shirt, tactical pants-wearing, generic Oakley-clad veterans. Usually with a Monster Energy drink coagulating in their unkempt goatees. And why are they always standing next to a lime-green Dodge Challenger?

The walking veteran clichés. The "you're welcome for my service" crowd. Check out my tongue-in-cheek analysis of the vet bro/bro vet crowd:

🌐 *https://vetbro.adambraatz.com*

The Low-Risk Entrepreneur

Brand development coaches and life-changing course salesmen are a dime a dozen on LinkedIn. These folks act as if there's only one way to achieve fulfillment and happiness—their way. And their proprietary knowledge is worth a pretty penny. While there are coaches and courses worth their weight in gold, this is not the norm. If you truly believe that a personal entrepreneurship, business, or branding coach is what you need to succeed, there's nothing wrong with that.

When shopping around, however, be on the lookout for common threads between you and them. Did they overcome adversity like you're currently facing? Do they have personal or anecdotal experience with your situations or similar situations? Or did their entrepreneurial journey begin as a debt-free millionaire? It sure is easy for people like that to evangelize "taking the leap" and ditching their nine-to-five, but they aren't likely to understand the complexities of your world. Not everyone can just up and leave their jobs to chase entrepreneurial dreams, and entrepreneurism is not the right fit for everyone. I made a post about it that I believe express my feelings on the matter quite perfectly.

Adam Braatz
I Empower Veterans to Thrive Through Professional Network, Branding, a...
6mo · Edited · 🌐

Not everyone can just up and leave their jobs to chase an entrepreneurial dream.

✗ If you voluntarily forfeited a $200,000+/year gig...

✗ If you are completely debt free with a decent nest egg saved up...

✗ If you don't have dependents...

Good for you! Nothing wrong with any of that.

But talking to the unemployed, underemployed, overworked, or over burdened like the only thing holding them back is their ambition or fortitude is insanely tone deaf.

Risk is inherent in all entrepreneurial endeavors, of course, but not all risk is created equal. Your risk in 'taking the leap' to entrepreneurship is not the same as others'.

I'm definitely not saying that the exhausted $40k/year earner with 7 kids and a mountain of debt is incapable of launching a successful business or service.

But their journey WILL be different than yours.

Sincerely,

Everyone who can't currently afford to drop everything to launch a business, much less spend $8000 on your coaching program to learn how some debt-free rich guy made it happen.

Early in my LinkedIn journey, I was pitched a three-month course and coaching plan from a non-veteran who lived halfway across the world—for a whopping $12,000. I'd been reading his content for quite some time and respected where he was coming from, so I was glad to hear him out. I tried to explain that while I was interested in what he had to say, it just wasn't feasible for me to borrow $12,000 at that moment. He chided me and disconnected. Incredibly, four years later, that same guy saw the above post, sent me a connection request, and then commented on the post in disagreement. Clearly, he'd forgotten about our exchange from four years prior and was probably zeroing in on another pitch attempt. I headed him off.

CHAPTER 11 | BE YOURSELF (DON'T BE "THAT PERSON")

He even "liked" his own post. Cringe. He voiced his displeasure to my reply publicly and blocked me in my DMs. Definitely don't be that person.

The Self-Licking Ice Cream Cone Person

If someone's attempting to sell a course that teaches people how to sell courses to folks who need courses, and so on, they're a self-licking ice cream cone. Same goes for if they're trying to coach you on how to coach clients who want to learn about coaching clients. You get the idea. Ask yourself, "Is the end result of the program or service a finite solution? Or is it an ongoing series of solutions for problems manifested by the originator?" Don't get sucked in by these people, and don't be the person who tries to generate profit without providing any real value.

The Side Hustle to Career Evangelist

Not everyone wants or needs a side hustle. Sometimes, folks with side hustles are perfectly content keeping their side hustles, well, on the side. The Side Hustle to Career Evangelist acts as if the only plausible path to success is to start a side hustle and scale it to the point where you can quit your day job. This particular path simply isn't realistic for everyone. Sure, it can be the dream for some, but anyone touting a one-size-fits-all approach to success is worthy of skepticism.

If someone's only solution to your unique problems is to "start a side hustle and then scale it," they just aren't being practical or rational. This is especially true in regard to your military transition. There are transition coaches and advice-givers around every corner. The military is exceptionally diverse, and every veteran's journey is different, but I don't need to tell you that. Just have your radar up for these people, and if you do find success and fulfillment in scaling a side hustle, don't be that person about it.

The No-Boundaries Creeper

I've had a few connections turn into No-Boundaries Creepers. This happens frequently when someone fails to read social cues or miscalculates their own professional equity. More on professional equity in the next section. Tagging someone in every single post you make or lighting up their DMs with novel-length messages can be really disrespectful. Please understand everyone's time is valuable, and you aren't entitled to any of it. If you aren't getting responses that you deem adequate, or any replies at all, don't harass the person. Read the room. Take the hint and back off.

This is not the time to put your detective skills to the test. Don't look up their phone number, home address, or send them weird emails voicing your disappointment in their lack of engagement. It could be that the person is crazy busy or going through something challenging. It could be that you are overwhelming them, and they need to take a break from you—which is perfectly valid and should be respected. You could be freaking them out a bit. Speaking as someone who has been on the receiving end of all of the above, I can tell you that these kinds of exchanges can devolve from discourteous to annoying to terrifying pretty quickly. Definitely never be this person.

The Clout-Tagger

There are those who tag twenty-five or so people in the body or comments section of each of their posts. The (flawed) logic behind that is that the tagees will see the post and engage with it, which will push it to a larger audience. The unfortunate reality is that this approach usually has the opposite effect. If you tag someone and they engage with your post, it will get a boost, which is a good thing. On the flip side, if you tag someone and they don't engage, it will seriously hurt the reach of that post. It's also bad etiquette that can become awfully annoying for the tagees, especially those with larger networks and influence on the platform. Influencers get over a thousand notifications each day from clout chasers. They don't appreciate it. Only tag someone if there is a legitimate reason to do so. Otherwise, don't be that person.

The Cut-and-Paster

These folks see a post garnering viral attention and just cut and paste, claiming it as their own. First of all, just because a post is taking off for someone else with their network doesn't mean it will resonate with yours or will align with your personal brand. Second, plagiarism is never acceptable. If you get caught stealing content just one time, it could permanently destroy your credibility. I can sniff out a cut-and-pasted post pretty easily. Here's a tip. If you suspect plagiarism, just copy the body text of the post and paste it into your search bar. LinkedIn will show you a list of how many times that exact same text has been used and by whom. Avoid those people. And don't be that person.

The Fake Story Attention Grabber

This type of person flat-out fabricates stories or situations to either elicit engagement or humblebrag. A popular example from back in the day was a first-person account of a boss who claimed to hire a young kid with no experience. The kid was late for their interview but ended up being a great asset to the company. Sure, it was a valuable and heartwarming lesson. But aside from the person who posted it for the first time ever—who even knows who that was—the other thousands of people on LinkedIn who were making the same claim were probably fabricating it. Don't be the person who makes stuff up for attention.

Keep an eye out for the scam bot version of the Not-So-Subtle Self-Promoter. These typically manifest as comments from 3rd-degree connections with a link. Often they will be accompanied by a realistic looking — but entirely fake — screen capped post from a celebrity endorsing a scam product through a link or suggested search term. These days, the celebrity most frequently impersonated and misquoted is Elon Musk.

These scams are mostly automated, so don't waste your time shouting down the perpetrator. If a comment like this shows up on a post of your, delete and report, then pat yourself on the back. These usually only pop up when you're getting good traction on a piece of content.

The Not-So-Subtle Self-Promoter

These parasites will hop into the comments sections of popular posts and share their own content in hopes of getting some piggyback traffic, no matter how unrelated. "Thanks for sharing this amazing post about best practices in hiring and supporting labor-wage employees. You may be interested in this article I wrote about cool airplanes." Don't do that.

Some people will also take a similar approach with new connections in their direct message inbox. "I see that you are an HR professional. I think you would like my recent blog post about puppies. Please share with your network." Those people are clearly takers and should be avoided. And, you guessed it, don't be that person.

The LinkedIn Police Officer

I touched on the LinkedIn Police Officer briefly earlier in this section. Look, I agree that LinkedIn is a platform designed first and foremost for professionals, career-seekers, and business connections. That said, social platforms are always expressions of how they are being used by the people active within their ecosystems. And that evolves over time. LinkedIn has changed immensely over the years. As long as someone is using a platform within the rules and regulations of the community guidelines set by that platform, let it go.

It's now more common than ever to see content that is not directly or even tangentially related to business or careers on LinkedIn. When this happens, there is invariably someone who chimes in with something like, "LinkedIn is a business platform. This kind of post doesn't belong here," or "This post belongs on Facebook." These LinkedIn Police became so prevalent and obnoxious a few years back that I made the following graphic, which I use as a canned reply whenever some barmy old square attempts to crash my LinkedIn party.

Do these people honestly think that comments of this nature accomplish anything other than making them look like inflexible old codgers? At a minimum, LinkedIn policing adds no value whatsoever and could seriously annoy other users, so don't waste your breath. Your comments can do very little to change how hundreds of millions of people choose to use LinkedIn, and an attempt to do so would be like trying to bail out the Titanic with a bucket. Don't be this person.

CHAPTER 12

LinkedIn Copywriting Fundamentals

Have you ever received a completely unreadable email from your commander? Picture an email consisting of one giant paragraph with an abundance of unnecessary fluff. What do you do when you receive something like that? Personally, I'm likely to skim, ignore, or put in my "read later," which is really my "read never" pile.

Alternatively, what are the components of a streamlined, readable email? For me, emails that are not too long and are composed of either bullet points or otherwise visually separated main ideas do the trick. It inspires an immediate response when appropriate. Military folks often laud the "bottom line up front" (BLUF) approach to written communications. It establishes the point quickly and succinctly with the most important details at the top and lets everyone go about their day. You must approach the copy—another word for the text-based portion of your communications—of any post with these same principles in mind.

LinkedIn used to limit text posts to 1300 characters but recently expanded that to a whopping 3000 characters. On average, that means you have nearly 500 words worth of space to work with, which is nearly equivalent to the length of a short blog article. Don't be fooled into believing that "more is more," as we still must establish and drive a point home in as targeted a fashion as is possible.

I developed the following infographic to get content newbies started out on the right foot. None of these rules are set in stone but are preferable to the one-giant-paragraph-of-unreadable-fluff approach. These guidelines apply to copy that you write on LinkedIn for a post of any kind, whether the text sits alone or accompanies an image, link, or video. Copywriting best practices are slightly different for each social platform. Having a firm understanding of these idiosyncrasies will set you up for success across the board. Later in this section, I'll share a few examples of quality posts and the characteristics that set them apart.

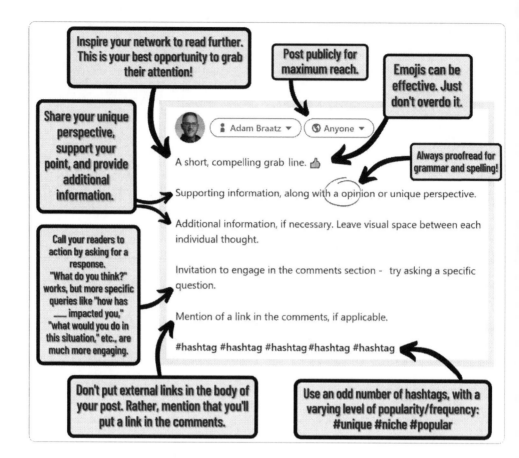

GRAB LINES

Grab lines are the most important part of your posts. They attract a reader's attention. They make casual scrollers curious to know more. It takes practice and a lot of trial and error to become proficient at writing quality grab lines.

If your post is more than 210 characters long, LinkedIn will cut off everything beyond the first couple lines and put a clickable "...see more" link, which expands the full body of the text when activated. The best grab lines seize a reader's attention and hit the 210-character limit on a cliffhanger. After all, when readers click "...see more," it makes the algorithm gods very happy. Additionally, if you haven't written something worthy of a reader's rapt attention within the first 210 characters, you need to restructure your post. It doesn't do you any good to have the most compelling, engagement-inducing part of your text buried behind a "...see more" wall.

SUPPORTING IDEAS

The section following your grab line is where you can expand upon your initial idea and share your unique perspectives about the topic. Though this is the portion of your post where you will delve deeper, take care not to pontificate. Your reader's attention is fickle and fleeting. Just because you have successfully captured it does not mean that your reader is committed to your post for the long haul. No matter how incredible your grab line is, following it with a lengthy paragraph of yawn-worthy text is a great way to inspire your LinkedIn network to click away and scroll on. Present your supporting points in a streamlined fashion while still maintaining good grammar and syntax. Your original LinkedIn posts are not an appropriate place for Internet shorthand.

CALLS TO ACTION

In the product and service marketing world, a call to action (CTA) inspires viewers and readers to enter a purchase pipeline of some kind. They have a broader application in the social media world. In this instance, a CTA is any tactic used to get viewers or readers to engage with your content. The more your audience reads, reacts to, shares, or comments on your content, the more LinkedIn will push it to wider audiences. Not all CTAs are created equal.

⊛ Cheap CTAs: Obvious engagement grabs, these annoy most LinkedIn users. In most circumstances, I'd choose no CTA over a cheap one. Though I confess, I have been guilty of a few myself. They often garner a high level of engagement due to their click-baity nature, but remember, quality is always better than quantity. Example: "Click the like reaction if you think cats are great!"

⊛ Mega-Cheap CTAs: These were in vogue on LinkedIn not too long ago and inspired massive—but entirely valueless—engagement. They were so prevalent and obnoxious that I created and posted the following satirical graphic. It was met with mixed reviews. Some people commented asking for clarification, others reacted in a disturbingly non-ironic way. Either way, the post got a fair amount of traction but provided no real value to anyone—aside from the brilliant few who got the joke— proving my point. Perhaps, I was ahead of my time with this one.

- ✴ **Command CTAs:** A form of Cheap CTAs, these are a bit more directive and, accordingly, more obnoxious. Nobody likes being told what to do, especially by a stranger on social media. Be careful with these. Example: "Tell me how many cats you own in the comments."

- ✴ **Short Question CTAs:** In my humble estimation, these are the lowest bar for an acceptable CTA. Short Question CTAs are quick and nonspecific. Examples: "What do you think?" or "Do you agree?"

- ✴ **Good CTAs:** These are better than Short Question CTAs because they're a bit more specific and conversational. Examples: "I'd love to know your thoughts about the whole cats vs. dogs thing." "Let's settle this once and for all: cats or dogs?" "Why are dogs so much better than cats?" Or finally, "What do you think—is it true that dog owners are cooler than cat owners?"

HASHTAGS

In 2019, LinkedIn seemed to prefer posts using exactly three hashtags. In 2022, rumor has it that five is the ideal. Either way, the sweet spot appears to be more than three but less than ten. Use an odd number of tags—five, seven, or nine—with varying lengths and popularity. Some should be specific to your product, brand, or niche (#tipsbyadam), while others should be more broad (#linkedintips).

HYBRID CONSIDERATIONS

Hashtags are not unique to LinkedIn. In fact, LinkedIn users were fairly late to the hashtag-adoption party. Hashes dominate platforms like Twitter and Instagram, and many of the hashtag best practices discussed in the section apply across the board.

Recently, Instagram advised creators to use between three to five hashtags, despite allowing for up to thirty, which came as a shock to many. **But whenever a platform drops hints about their content distribution algorithms, take their advice seriously and act accordingly.** *Here are some suggested hashtag numbers for other platforms:*

Twitter: *no more than two*
Facebook: *two to three*
TikTok: *no more than five*
YouTube: *three to five; the first three tags in the description will also be displayed above the video title.*

If you're looking for ideas, try hashtags that are location, industry, campaign, or community-based. This aspect of content on LinkedIn is highly speculative and not entirely reliable. I went years without adding a single hashtag to my LinkedIn content and did just fine, so feel free to experiment, but don't hang your hat on them.

SOME ADDITIONAL RULES OF THUMB:

⊛ Make sure your post accessibility is set to "anyone." There are some rare circumstances where you may want to have a post viewed only by your existing network but, for the most part, you'll want the widest possible reach.

⊛ Leave visual space between your grab line, supporting ideas, and CTA. I try to stick with around two sentences per section with an occasional single sentence for emphasis. But that's only when I want an idea to stand out on its own. As with emails, a single giant chunk of text turns people off.

⊛ Visual space between individual ideas is good. But avoid "broetry." This is the practice of spreading your post out to the max by leaving visual space between each and every single sentence.

⊛ Emojis are fun and can be effective—just don't overdo them. I typically put a single emoji in my grab line and maybe one or two more throughout the post at a maximum.

⊛ If there's an external source you want to link to, avoid putting it in the body of your post. There's evidence that external links hinder the overall reach of a post. I mean, LinkedIn wants to keep you on LinkedIn doing LinkedIn things with LinkedIn users, right? A way to avoid this while still sharing the external source is to write something like, "Link in comments" in the body of your post, then share the link as a comment below.

⊛ Proofread like your life depends on it. If you make an egregious spelling or grammar mistake, you have the opportunity to edit the copy after the fact. Unfortunately, there are indications that editing a post after posting may displease the algorithm gods and may stunt your reach potential. Edit when you must, but do so sparingly. It's always best to make sure your post is right the first time around.

⊛ Use punctuation, good grammar, and proper syntax. No acronyms. I'm talking to you, veterans.

CHECK IT OUT!

Download your own high resolution copy of my "Perfect LinkedIn Post" formula by visiting The Thriving Veteran online community:

🌐 *https://community.adambraatz.com*

THE ANATOMY OF GOOD LINKEDIN COPY

Here are a few examples of text-based posts that, at the time, garnered engagement at a rate higher than my average. Whenever you have a post break out, it's best to go back and analyze what set it apart and determine a set of best practices that work for you and your network. It may seem like a random occurrence, but things rarely go viral by accident. Something about the post resonated with people in one way or another.

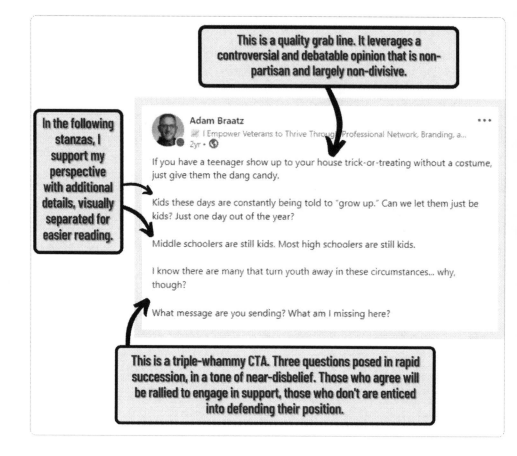

This post has generated such entertaining results that I do it, or something very similar, every single year around Halloween. In 2021, I presented it as a poll—which we'll discuss later in this section—and due to the overwhelmingly viral nature of poll-based content on LinkedIn at the time, nearly broke the Internet.

Adam Braatz
I Empower Veterans to Thrive Through Professional Network, Branding, a...
1mo • 🌐

I lost my temper and yelled at my son last night. He's over it, but I'm not.

I feel absolutely wretched. I keep picturing the look on his face. 😟

Look, I totally acknowledge that some situations call for a bit of escalation. This wasn't one of those situations.

He's 4. Kids that age straight up aren't capable of being rational, especially if they're already worked up about something. The way I reacted to his behavior simply wasn't fair.

Plus, it solved absolutely nothing. He needed patience, empathy, and understanding from me in that moment, and I failed miserably.

I mean, is that seriously all the patience I could muster for him? For a little dude who I love with every single fiber of my heart? Come on, man.

When things calmed down, I held him and said "the way I reacted was not appropriate, or fair. I shouldn't have yelled at you. Adults make mistakes, too, and it's really important to be able to admit it and apologize. I was wrong, and I'm really sorry bud."

I hope he remembers that part of the whole encounter.

When I was a kid, parents were infallible and rarely apologized to their kids, but I hope that is starting to change. Humility, honesty, integrity... it all lends to our credibility and builds trust.

Have you ever genuinely humbled yourself to your kids?

If you create a post this long, you'd better use one heck of a grab line. The above landed very well due to the vulnerable and relatable nature of mine. If you can encourage a random scroller to stop and read a lengthier piece of content, you'll likely gain higher-than-average traction. Remember, dwell time is a huge contributor to greater reach potential, and the algorithm gods give you a leg up when a reader clicks on "…see more."

GOOD COPY WITHOUT A CTA

You don't necessarily need a CTA to encourage your connections to chime in. The following two posts do not have any overt CTAs but were forceful enough to have inspired greater-than-normal engagement.

Adam Braatz
🪁 I Empower Veterans to Thrive Through Professional Network, Branding, a...
9mo • Edited • 🌐

If you have a problem with my 4 year-old son briefly interrupting our Zoom meeting, because he just wants to see what I'm up to or say hello, you can go fly a kite. 🪁

I mean it.

There is no meeting, connection, business deal, or job that is more important to me than making my son feel heard, seen, validated, appreciated, or respected.

If you want to do business with me, connect with me, whatever -- that's part of the deal. There is a chance my son will pop in and say hello. He may introduce himself or show you a picture he's drawn.

He's as respectful as a 4 year-old can be regarding the work I do from home, and never takes more than a minute or two.

You simply cannot win in a battle for priority.

Sorry; not sorry. 🐨

Be careful with posts like this. Though they are an essential part of establishing who you are to your digital audience, put deliberate thought into which subjects you wish to draw a line in the sand over.

Adam Braatz
☑ I Empower Veterans to Thrive Through Professional Network, Branding, a...
8mo · 🌐

I had a rough day yesterday.

A pretty significant disappointment with my personal business launched me into a downward spiral of self doubt and negativity. I simply couldn't shake it.

I'm not sharing this to throw a public pity party, or to solicit encouraging feedback. Hear me out:

I'm sharing because I want you to know that all of us experience doubt, especially when faced with failure or seemingly insurmountable challenges.

If you've ever felt that way, you aren't alone.

I still believe in my heart that the only way to truly fail is to give up. Tenacity and grit when times are tough separate the winners from the rest.

If you're out there grinding and wondering if or when it will all be worth it: don't give up. You could be on the verge of a breakthrough.

I believe in you. Go get 'em!

Despite a distinct lack of a CTA, this post garnered higher-than-average attention for three reasons: it has a great grab line, it's vulnerable/authentic, and it's uplifting/aspirational.

HYBRID CONSIDERATIONS

Your carefully-curated content deserves to have a good, long life. It would be a shame for it to exist in that one moment, only to die in obscurity a short while later. Get the maximum mileage out of your original content by repurposing it on other platforms. You will need to alter the content for each platform, though, because each has slightly different rules and dialects.

Some creators utilize content management software to share their posts across multiple platforms at the same time. Unless the program allows you to tweak the post for each specific platform, I would avoid this approach. It's easy to tell when someone is merely sharing content from another platform. It looks distinctly out of place and comes off as tacky and lazy. Post natively on each platform, especially as you are getting started on your brand-building journey.

After all, the only way to truly become comfortable with any platform is to get into the trenches with it.

CHAPTER 13

Beyond the Text Post

VISUAL IMAGE POSTS

Posts with images attached can be extremely effective—as long as they're executed correctly. Adding an image to your post will not guarantee improved engagement. Never add an image unless there's a relevant, tactical purpose. An image can be effective as the main focal point of the post or in support of the copy. Either way, there are a few rules to keep in mind:

⊛ An image should always enhance what you're trying to convey and represent the central theme of your post or directly support it.

⊛ Resist the temptation to use generic, unrelated free-license stock images just because you can.

⊛ Though LinkedIn technically allows you to post an image on its own without any text, I advise against it in most circumstances. There should be written copy either supporting or explaining the picture, and it should follow the same text-based post rules as outlined above.

⊛ Images must be high quality and high resolution. Sharing grainy, pixelated, low-resolution photos may harm the overall impression of your brand. Lower quality imagery can be acceptable in candid circumstances but only if absolutely essential to the story.

⊛ Images that appear to be of higher resolution on smaller screens, like your smartphone, don't always look good on larger screens. Ideally, your image size should be at least 1080x1080. Verify that everything looks good on a desktop monitor, too, before going about your day.

⊛ You have the option to post multiple images in a sequence—see the example below—which LinkedIn will organize into a neat collage for you. This is not, however, a Facebook photo album and should not be treated as such. The images need to be variable enough to justify having more than one and be related in a way that's essential to your story. Multiple images that show the progression of a personal endeavor or project are extremely effective.

ANATOMY OF A QUALITY IMAGE POST

This may easily be my best LinkedIn post of all time. The four-word grab line cuts like a knife. It's humble yet aspirational and inspirational. It shows triumph over adversity and personal accomplishment without humblebragging. It also includes my son, who is super cool. And adding a family element makes me appear human and relatable. Some parents elect not to share photographs of their children on social media for safety and security reasons. I do so sparingly. At the time, I was beyond shocked that this post took off like it did, but in hindsight, it makes perfect sense. I learned a lot from analyzing its trajectory. Always take the time to do a thorough after-actions debrief when something strikes a chord or, conversely, bombs massively.

CAROUSEL POSTS

Carousel posts are one of the most powerful and underutilized formats that LinkedIn currently offers. Rather than presenting multiple images in a collage, as explained above, carousel posts allow users to flip through a series of images, almost like a slideshow. For example, this is image 3 of 7 in a great carousel post by Gary Vaynerchuk.

Many users find themselves dumbfounded when trying to create a carousel post. I'll tell you the secret. You must use a PDF file with each page as an individual image. For all of you savvy Canva users out there, the process is as simple as selecting PDF as the format when downloading a multi-slide project. Ensure that the grab line in your body of text is solid, as usual, but also treat the first image in the sequence as if it were a grab line in itself. If it encourages your readers to engage to see more, you'll get bonus algorithm points for the clicks as well as the dwell time.

LINKEDIN'S NATIVE BLOG PUBLISHER

Not everyone has their own website or blog. The truth is that most people who have one don't need one. Regardless, it's important for us to put pen to paper whenever possible and share our thoughts and expertise with the world. It's incredible how many people are unaware that LinkedIn has a built-in blog publishing tool, which is an ideal place to share said thoughts and expertise without going through the hassle of launching a new website or blog from scratch.

In my experience, blog articles written through LinkedIn's native publisher can garner unpredictable and underwhelming reach. Generally speaking, you will get lower-than-normal engagement and reach with LinkedIn articles. You may be asking, "Why on earth someone would want to write one then?"

First of all, you can and should link to the article from outside sources, just like you would a blog article that resides on your personal web page or, if you have one, your Medium account. If you're not familiar with this site, according to Medium, they're "a platform where readers find dynamic thinking, and where expert and undiscovered voices can share their writing on any topic." Next, linking from outside sources is less expensive—meaning free—and less labor intensive than establishing your own website or blog. Finally, and most importantly, you can put the article in the "Featured Content" section of your personal profile. This will add to the overall visual completion of your profile and tell visitors that you care enough about your industry or discipline to take the time to write about it.

Accordingly, I suggest that everyone write one article if only for the express purpose of having it as the first item in the "Featured Content" section of their profiles. To get started, head to your newsfeed via your desktop browser—this feature is not currently available via the mobile app—and look for "Write Article" nestled on the right side of the "Start a Post" entry box in the middle column of your newsfeed. Book out an hour or two and get down to business.

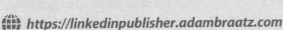

There's no need to go overboard here. If you have a 5000-word masterpiece in you, then by all means go for it, but a much shorter article of four or five paragraphs will do the trick—especially if you space things out with a couple high quality images. Write about your industry, discipline, or your ideas about the industry or discipline you are aspiring to transition into. Are there challenges facing others in this occupation? Do you have insights about what the future of your industry looks like? Is there a solution out there that people aren't seeing or adopting? Write about those sorts of things.

Though serious writers find the idea blasphemous, the unfortunate truth is that the title of your article matters as much as the content. If you don't believe me, consider what kind of titles and headlines get the most clicks. The content doesn't matter if nobody is interested enough to click and learn more. Then think of how often articles are shared based on the title and thumbnail photo alone by folks who haven't read a single word of it, especially with articles of a political nature. Once you start to wrap your brain around the art of title and headline optimization, you won't be able to help analyzing every title you see. It's a blessing and a curse. To make matters a bit more confusing, LinkedIn is currently calling titles "Headlines." Don't be confused. They're the same thing. Your LinkedIn article will also be searchable in Google—a huge opportunity—based on the keywords and clickability of your title/headline. Many influencers even advise aspiring content creators to start by writing an optimized headline before doing anything else.

Effective blog writing is worth a book of its own, so I won't get too deep in the weeds here. Below are a few quick tips to make sure your first LinkedIn article is solid:

Title/Headline:

⊛ Keep your title/headline between 50-60 characters.

⊛ Put your most desirable keywords toward the beginning when possible.

⊛ Asking a question—who/what/where/when/why/how—makes the headline more clickable.

- ✴ Numbered lists are also desirable. But always use odd numbers. 5 Reasons Why Dogs are Better Than Cats.

- ✴ Use a high-resolution photo at the top. Free-license stock images are usually acceptable in this scenario.

Body:

- ✴ Use headings to visually break up main ideas.

- ✴ Avoid excessively long paragraphs.

- ✴ Use an image or two through the body to add interest to your content.

- ✴ Always end with some kind of CTA.

- ✴ Ask someone you trust—a colleague, mentor, friend, or spouse—take a look before you hit "Publish." Bad grammar and syntax can have a huge negative impact on your overall professional presentation.

Once everything looks good and you're ready to share your new article with the world, smash the "Publish" button at the top of the page. LinkedIn will immediately prompt you to share the article with your network in an original post, which you should definitely do. Bear in mind that you'll need to generate copy for this share, and using the methods outlined above for text posts will ensure it has the best chance to reach more people.

CHECK IT OUT!

Writing click-worthy titles for your blogs or YouTube videos is an art form. I use CoSchedule software to help me optimize my titles before I do anything else! Check out how I do it:

🌐 *https://headlines.adambraatz.com*

VIDEO CONTENT

The demand for online video content has been on a steady rise since the birth of YouTube in 2005. In the product marketing world, it's nearly impossible to scale a brand to international name recognition without the use of video content. In 2019, Cisco predicted that 82% of all global Internet traffic will come from video streaming and downloads, which is insane.

The algorithm gods smile upon those who use a greater variety of LinkedIn's features, so consider adding some semblance of video to your content repertoire. As always, it's important to do it the right way. Some people struggle mightily with recording themselves and sharing it online. I get it. Really, I do. But hang in there. Usually, those who tighten up at the thought of putting themselves out there in video format relax a bit when I tell them the rules. It isn't as complicated or stressful as you'd think. You aren't producing a feature film here. I'll share some of the most common questions I get about LinkedIn video content best practices below.

How long should my video be?

Short. It should be short. Nobody has the time to listen to a fifteen-minute soliloquy from any of their connections, much less from a stranger. Get to the point quickly, provide value, and close it out. Save the long-form content for your YouTube channel or Instagram Video (IGTV), if at all.

How do I get and keep viewers' attention?

Think of your opening dialogue like a grab line in a text-based post. You have a maximum of three seconds to get your audience's attention to suck them in. Preparation is your friend. I like to write an outline to make sure I cover all the important points, but I never write out the full dialogue for fear of sounding robotic. Extemporaneous speaking is the way to go, always.

How much time should I spend producing the video?

There's no need to learn complicated video editing or production software. Most smartphones will do the trick to get you started with your video journey. If you have video production chops, feel free to use them, but don't go overboard. You don't want your video content to look like a cheesy billboard, and you don't want a lengthy intro with credits, music, and links either—folks will click away because they don't feel like waiting ten seconds for the actual valuable content to show up. Sad, but true.

Do I need to buy any gear?

Generally speaking, no, but there are a few inexpensive items that can increase the production quality of your video content exponentially—a cheap, flexible tripod to hold your phone steady while you record and a small ring light of some kind.

How do I get set up?

Check the video recording settings on your device, and ensure that you are capturing content in 1080p or higher if possible. Do a test shot or use a stand-in to make sure you're framed up in the shot, not too far away, and not too close. If you feel as if you're slightly too close to your recording device, you're likely right in the sweet spot. Work in a space with ample lighting, but don't work directly underneath a lighting source or against a plain wall because it creates unflattering shadows. Ring lights help here, projected at an angle so as not to reflect in your eyes or glasses.

Eliminate any background noise, static, or humming appliances and speak clearly. Do your best to look directly into the camera when you speak. This is something I struggle with. Practice helps.

Do I need captions?

While you're technically allowed to post without captions, I would advise against it. Not having captions produces a barrier for viewers who are scrolling without their audio on. Depending on your industry, captions can also be required to comply with the law as outlined in the Americans with Disabilities Act.

Luckily, LinkedIn allows you to add caption files after the fact by clicking on the edit icon in the corner of the post. And its Live Video—which we'll discuss below— auto-dictates captions while you're speaking, which is very handy. There are also third-party apps that will take care of transcribing your speech and will let you download the captions to add to the video.

What is a thumbnail, and why should I care?

The picture shown while your video sits idle is called the thumbnail. LinkedIn will let you upload whatever you want to be the thumbnail on the same screen where you would upload an external caption file. If you do not provide LinkedIn with a thumbnail, it will default to using whatever content exists in the very first frame of the video. So if you were to start your video with a produced fade in from black, the preview thumbnail would be completely black, which does little to grab the attention of a newsfeed passerby.

If you aren't planning on doing any production or creating an image to use as a custom thumbnail, then think about where you want the video's first frame to be. Press record or trim the video to start at a point when you are in the frame, facing the camera, smiling, and about to speak.

I've produced a great video that I would love to share with my LinkedIn network. I've already uploaded it onto YouTube. Should I share the YouTube link on LinkedIn or upload the video file directly?

This is a million-dollar question with strong opinions on both sides. Amateur algorithm scientists will tell you that LinkedIn hates the links that take its users to an external site and will throttle the content accordingly. On the flip side, LinkedIn definitely doesn't give the same boost to native videos as it did when it first allowed them on its platform back in 2017.

My advice is to do both. Make a post uploading the video natively on LinkedIn, then a couple of weeks later, make a new post which shares a link to that same video but on YouTube. Analyze which approach resonates best with your network. Put that information into your pocket for the future. It should go without saying that in both cases the video/link should be accompanied by an engaging chunk of attention-worthy copy. Ask yourself which approach resonated better with your audience, and use the answer to decide how you share content in the future.

How do I do a Live Video stream?

LinkedIn currently requires approval to use its Live Video feature. Additionally, LinkedIn does not have native Live Video capabilities and requires you to work through a 3rd party streaming service like Streamyard. You don't need to have an absolutely massive platform to gain approval, but there are a few criteria you must meet before LinkedIn will give you its blessings.

FROM LINKEDIN.COM:

To maintain a safe and trusted environment on LinkedIn, we grant broadcast access to members and Pages based on a set of criteria. All criteria must be met for an access request to be approved. The criteria for Live Video access are:

Audience base – Members and Pages with more than 150 followers and/or connections are eligible to be evaluated for LinkedIn Live access.

Recent shares of original content (any type) - We look for members and Pages who have experience creating original content on LinkedIn (For example, creating posts with text, images, or videos, publishing articles, etc.) to evaluate if they will be able to make the most of LinkedIn Live.

A history of abiding by our Professional Community Policies - We want to ensure our members have a safe, trusted, and professional experience on LinkedIn, as defined by our Professional Community Policies. Only members, Pages, and their admins that have a good standing record will be considered for Live Video access.

Geography – LinkedIn Live is not available at this time for members and Pages based in mainland China.

If you believe you meet this criteria, you can:

1. Auto-apply if you'll be going live using certain third-party broadcast tools.

2. Turn on Creator Mode on your LinkedIn profile for access to creator tools.

3. Create an event on LinkedIn to generate an automatic check to see whether you are eligible. If you are, you will be able to choose LinkedIn Live in the event format drop-down.

All three pathways above will perform the same check to see whether you meet our access criteria. Only members and Pages who've received access via one of the pathways can become LinkedIn Live broadcasters.

If you do not meet one or more of our criteria, we will not grant you access. If you would like to be reconsidered, you can check again after 30 days, if you feel that your status has changed.

How do I make a successful livestream on LinkedIn?

All the rules for video content found above apply for livestreaming video as well, with the exception of duration. People expect live video presentations to be longer, with the added element of interacting with your viewers. You still need to get to the point quickly, though, and as with above, preparation is the key. I again suggest using an outline and speaking off the cuff. Most streaming platforms have a built-in countdown timer you can use. For the love of all that is holy in this world, do NOT use it! Why? Because 95% of your audience will not hang around for thirty seconds to see what comes next. You've already lost them by that point. By the time you start with your presentation, they've already been watching something else for twenty-seven seconds.

CHECK IT OUT!

I personally use Streamyard for all of my live streaming videos and love it! Try it out for free:

 https://streamyard.com?fpr=adamb

What was that 30-day challenge you mentioned earlier all about?

The 30-day video challenge is a great way to jumpstart your LinkedIn video creation journey. In essence, you publicly commit to posting one short video on a different topic every day for 30 days. Your first video should be an announcement about the challenge. The key to being successful is to plan ahead and be vigilant about only sharing high quality content. I've done this twice. Each time, I've seen my network explode as a result. But it isn't for the faint of heart. The commitment to doing the full 30 days is nothing to shake a stick at.

EVENTS

LinkedIn launched an Events platform in 2019. I've found using LinkedIn's Events platform yields varying results, but as is the case with most things, it depends on how much targeted effort you put into it. While it conveniently allows you to invite your network connections to your event or livestream in bulk, be cautious, as each invite counts toward your outgoing invite total. I learned this lesson the hard way! Folks who RSVP in the affirmative to the event will be notified when it starts, which is especially handy for livestreams. Targeted outreach for invitations is the way to go here.

> **FROM LINKEDIN.COM:**
>
> *"The LinkedIn Events feature provides members with an easy way to create and join professional Events that interest them, such as meetups, online workshops, seminars, and more. LinkedIn members can use the feature to find and join communities, grow their business, network with others, and learn new skills."*

It's important to note that scheduling a livestream via third-party software will automatically create an event, which can be handy. Make sure all the content carried over from your third-party posts to the event page itself. You can—and should—add yourself and your guests, where applicable, as speakers for the event, and add additional details, show notes, or links.

STORIES AND OTHER NEW FEATURES

LinkedIn had a short-term affair with "Stories," which lasted less than a year before they pulled the plug. "Stories" are short-form videos that disappear after twenty-four hours, similar to the style of stories that Facebook and Instagram had famously borrowed from Snapchat. "Stories" simply didn't land with LinkedIn's audience. Unfortunately, most LinkedIn users who used this feature treated it like a billboard to shill their own products and services. LinkedIn promised to reevaluate and may bring a different iteration of it forward in the future, so keep an eye out.

LinkedIn has a "Groups" feature that has been on death's door for years despite a significant overhaul in 2019. LinkedIn Groups simply have not functioned as intended, and I predict they'll be removed or replaced in short order. I'm buddies with a couple people who swear by them, but I have not seen a widespread benefit. Don't take my word for it, though, try joining a "Group" and see for yourself. Have fun with the notifications.

LinkedIn recently launched a new "Newsletter" feature, and though I haven't used it myself, I have been bombarded with invitations to sign up for about a thousand of them from near-complete strangers and find that to be extremely obnoxious. At present, LinkedIn is set by default to send an invitation—to your entire network—to sign up for your newsletter when you launch it. Sending invitations in a nontargeted fashion goes against everything LinkedIn claims to stand for. There's nothing deliberate, intentional, or personal about a bulk invite. I hope they fix this flaw and soon. Curating a traditional email list is exceptionally important for your brand development, but I'm not sure if LinkedIn is right the platform to do it on. It remains to be seen, but I'm avoiding it for now.

Early in 2022, LinkedIn announced it would soon be unveiling a new podcast network, which I'm extremely excited about. Details are hard to come by at this point, however. In all likelihood, by the time this book is released, the feature will have launched, and there will be an abundance of information and resources available for it. So, I'll have to save that information for the second edition. Also be on the lookout for a live audio-only feature, similar to Clubhouse or Twitter's recently added Spaces. With the success of both Clubhouse and Twitter Spaces in the professional and business world, I would be shocked if LinkedIn didn't unveil its own competitor soon. It may or may not be integrated into the podcast network. Only time will tell.

Overall, the lesson here is that LinkedIn—heck, all social platforms—will evolve and grow over time. Consider the overwhelming onslaught of features available on Facebook these days. Speaking as someone who's used Facebook since it came to my university in the early 2000s—back then it was only available at certain schools, and you needed a *.edu (school) email address to access it—the evolution has been staggering. Always have your radar up for changes and new features, and don't be afraid to dive in. Sometimes being the first in the pool is enough to help you, your brand, or your business stand out.

SHARING IS CARING

Sharing articles or posts flippantly is encouraged—and disproportionately rewarded—on quick-fix platforms like Facebook and Twitter. LinkedIn's algorithm does not seem to hold the same affinity for sharing. For the sharer, it can be very challenging to gain traction or engagement on a shared post even when best practices are followed, which does little to encourage the practice.

This news can be utterly disheartening for those in industries, like banking and financing, that strictly regulate their employee's LinkedIn activity. I could write another book about how ridiculously shortsighted it is for companies to overregulate their employees' LinkedIn presence, but that's the corporate world for you. They'd much rather handcuff the people helping them build their empires than handle the occasional fallout from a foolish or misguided post. But I digress.

There are a few things that can be done to stack the deck in your favor when sharing others' original content.

✸ Always add your two cents

Don't just click "Share" and move on. This isn't a retweet. LinkedIn always affords you the opportunity to add copy, and you should, each and every time. Be sure to follow the same best practices for posting original text-based content. If you're in a strictly regulated industry, get clear guidance and clarification from your corporate communications team on what you can and can't do.

✸ Internal is (usually) better than external

LinkedIn wants to keep you active and engaged on LinkedIn. So, logically, it follows that shares from internal sources like LinkedIn-based articles or posts get priority over external shares to other blogs or YouTube videos. Though the odds are technically stacked against it, I have had external links go viral.

✸ If you have to share externally . . .

There is a way to half-post an external link. Although I get the impression that the LinkedIn algorithm has gotten wise to the practice—and again, we would be unwise to try to trick it—its use is still commonplace. Instead of sharing the link in the body of your post and allowing the auto-populate feature to do its work, write something like "link in comments below" and post the external link in the comments. There are varied reports of the efficacy of this approach, but as always, try different things to see what resonates best with your particular audience and network.

✸ The algorithm (kind of) hates trending news

In the upper right corner of your main feed page, there's a box titled "LinkedIn News," which shows trending topics and articles. When you click on it, you'll be taken to a blurb written by a LinkedIn-employed editor and shown a list of all content related to the subject. There's also a share button toward the top. Every time I've clicked on that share button, the result was entirely underwhelming. No traction or engagement whatsoever. On the other hand, whenever I've researched those same trending topics and made original posts sharing my thoughts related to those issues, they've done quite well. In other words, don't use "LinkedIn News" for sharable content—consider it market research.

We're currently living in a creator-centric and sharing-based economy, so always be on the lookout for new ways to share. For example, LinkedIn has been experimenting with a feature which allows users to share their own comment replies as new posts. I would say the closest relative to this feature is Twitter's "retweet with comment." Be willing to experiment with all of the different features available to you, and don't forget to take advantage of the algorithm boost that new features typically get when LinkedIn is trying to hype something up.

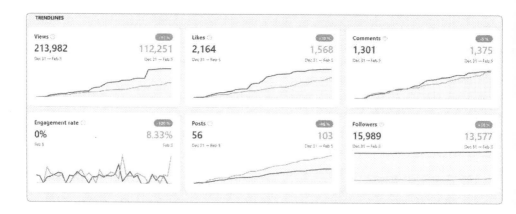

Knowledge is power when it comes to your content strategy. Unfortunately, despite a significant upgrade in 2022, LinkedIn has few built-in analytics tools for their users' personal profile. Those who turn on "Creator Mode" will have access to slightly deeper analytics on all their activity. Regardless, the only avenue for truly in-depth analytical tools is SHIELD. You don't need SHIELD when you're just getting started. But if you begin to get serious about your content and maximizing your reach, I strongly recommend it. I use it every day.

CHECK IT OUT!

Currently, the only place to get truly in-depth analytical tools is SHIELD. If you begin to get serious about your content and want to maximize your reach, I strongly recommend it.

Visit here for more info on SHIELD using my affiliate link to get the best deal:

🌐 *https://www.shieldapp.ai/?via=adam*

CHAPTER 14

Careers, Business, & Influence

"First off, I just want to say thank you for your service. We are huge supporters of the military around here. Unfortunately, I just don't see how your experience is relevant for this position."

I was floored. Did this guy even look at my résumé? Or had he seen I was a veteran and immediately written me off? My experience fit the position description perfectly, almost line-by-line, or so I'd thought. I started to realize why I'd heard many vets say they deliberately hid the fact that they'd served until after they got the job.

Little did I know at the time, but I was knee-deep in an ego-centric victim mentality and couldn't shake it. I'd missed an important lesson. This hiring manager could've had a subconscious prejudice against military members and their experiences as they pertain to civilian employment, sure, but the responsibility in this situation was mine. I'd clearly done an abysmal job of expressing the value I would bring to the organization as a civilian employee. Having a solid, relevant résumé was just one facet in a much, much bigger picture.

When the interviewer threw out the classic softball question, "Tell me about yourself," the first thing out of my mouth was, "I'm a veteran of the United States Air Force." I had a fresh high and tight. I was wearing shirt stays, for Pete's sake. I called the guy "sir." Nothing whatsoever about me "fit" there.

What I thought would convey the pinnacle of elite professionalism came off more like I'd wandered off base and into the interview by accident.

One afternoon, I was sitting in a meeting with two coworkers at my first place of employment after service. My supervisor and I were facilitating a friendly and totally pedestrian transition of responsibility for an event from us to the third participant in the meeting who ran another department. We were in a hurry, so I tried to get to the point, but I felt as if the overall vibe in the meeting was cheerful. I finished filling the other department lead in on the pertinents for the event and the logistics I'd already put into place.

And she hardened. "It sounds like you're trying to tell me how to do my job." She practically spit at me.

I looked at my supervisor, who appeared just as shocked and confused as I was.

Meanwhile, the woman continued, pointing a knobby finger right at my face. "I just saw it in you for the first time. You've tried to hide it, but I can see it clearly. The MILITARY in you. You just went military on me, and I feel attacked."

I had no idea what to say. In hindsight, I could've replied with something quippy to the effect of, "Look, lady, I was a basic training instructor. If I 'went military' on you, you'd be looking for a new pair of pants right now." But alas, I missed that golden—pun intended—opportunity. Instead, I spluttered. I apologized for coming off as confrontational and assured her that I was merely trying to get to business.

Once the shock of the situation wore off, I had a sobering thought. Replace the word "military" in her accusation with any other demographic, and you'd have a serious human resources issue on your hands. Why had she felt emboldened to make such a statement? Even more infuriating, she had a poster with a flag in her cubicle which proudly stated, "Support Our Troops." I realized at that moment the immense challenge facing veterans in the civilian workforce.

My supervisor, a civilian, backed me up and insisted that I'd been completely positive and professional, but the damage to my psyche had been done. I started to second guess nearly everything that I said or did. Did this lady honestly feel as if I were a ticking time bomb? A stereotypical drill-sergeant-type robot? Had she just been waiting for me to "go military" on her or someone else? Did the other folks in the office feel the same way about *me? Had I "gone military" on anyone else? Was any kindness, empathy, or positivity on my part seen as some disingenuous cover for whatever assumptions they had made about me? In short, yes and no. The reality was somewhere smack dab in the middle.*

I shared the above stories back-to-back to show the multiple challenges veterans face as they transition into the civilian workforce after service. Many veterans blame civilians for not understanding or appreciating the immense value and unique skills they bring to the table, while many civilians blame veterans for not fully integrating or failing to convey their value adequately. Some civilians feel as if veterans look down upon them. Many veterans face varying degrees of prejudice in the civilian workplace. Because of that, both hiring managers and employment seekers have a responsibility to adapt and get educated if they hope to reap the abundant mutual benefits of veteran employment.

While civilian hiring managers must acknowledge and combat their preexisting stereotypes about military service members, veterans need to learn how to "speak civilian." I've heard some vets say that they pretended they were wearing civilian camouflage, at least until they got comfortable. Even the word "camouflage" is military-esque vernacular, though, and could foster a thoroughly non-civilian mindset. Not only must we dress for the job we want, but we must talk the talk too.

Even though my experience and education were absolutely perfect for the position I was applying for in the first story, I hadn't spoken the hiring manager's language. He didn't "get it," and I was a fool for expecting him to see through the drill sergeant sitting in front of him. I was approaching employment as a "taker" rather than a "giver." I felt entitled to more effort from the hiring manager than I was willing to deliver myself. I wanted him to meet me in the middle but stayed firmly entrenched in my own endzone. The civilian working world is a tough beast. If you're looking for an opportunity as an employee or in a business-to-business transaction, you'd better wrap your brain around a "giver" mindset.

I said this earlier, but I feel the need to really foot-stomp this one. It's crucial to approach digital networking in a similar fashion as an in-person event, like a conference or an interview. Sure, your method of communication is simpler to execute online, but that shouldn't make your intent any less personal or personable. Though it's simpler to communicate through LinkedIn, for example, it's also easier to come across as a "taker."

As I also mentioned in the opening of this book, professional network development is not a priority topic for transition educators or facilitators, and it shows. Every single day, I see veterans leap into LinkedIn for the first time and make the same mistakes. You now have a technical, tactical understanding of profile optimization, LinkedIn network development, and content creation best practices. However, a strategic understanding of network development and professional equity is necessary to glue all of that together. Understanding these principles is essential for all professionals but even more urgent for military transitioners. You'll see why in a minute.

WHAT IS PROFESSIONAL EQUITY?

Professional equity is your total combined leverage as a professional, which includes your experience, skills, reputation, the size of your network, and your ability to influence your network to take action. All of these factors work in tandem and are nearly worthless on their own. There's no professional equity to be had, for example, in a giant network with millions of followers if you're unable to inspire or influence them. Nor do abundant skills and expertise matter if your reputation is not favorable. The higher your professional equity, the more power you'll have when searching for a new career, pitching products and services, and building a platform of influence. Unless a veteran gets ahead of the game and networks aggressively and deliberately as they're leading up to transitioning, they'll have next to zero professional equity in the civilian working world. This is regardless of rank, career field, or pedigree while in the service. But don't fret. It's never too late to get started. Additionally, there are advantages to starting out with a low professional equity.

Every endeavor or campaign a professional undertakes has what I like to call a "network polarity," either negative or positive. In essence, those with negative polarity are in need, and those with a positive polarity are in a position to provide. Neither is better than the other. Rather, both are needed to fulfill a transaction of goods, services, information, or inspiration. Much like neither end of a battery is better than the other, but both are needed to provide a charge. Check out the examples below.

Negative Polarities	Positive Polarities
business owner pitching to a contractor	manager in a position to sign B2B contracts
job seeker	hiring authority
entry-level sales or development associate	established professional with large network
new LinkedIn user	LinkedIn thought leader
professional seeking to build skillset	a subject-matter expert

In any given situation, it's absolutely essential to realistically assess our polarity—and the extent to which we are in either camp—in order to tweak our approach for maximum results. We often simultaneously hold different polarities in different areas. A popular social media influencer looking for a day job will have a positive network polarity in the social influence arena but a negative polarity when it comes to career. Military veterans tend to drastically miscalculate the extent of their professional equity as well as their network polarity. I've frequently seen lower ranking enlisted transitioners underestimate their post-service potential, while field-grade officers often struggle with a vast overestimation of theirs. Here are a few examples of the various combinations of professional equity and network polarity.

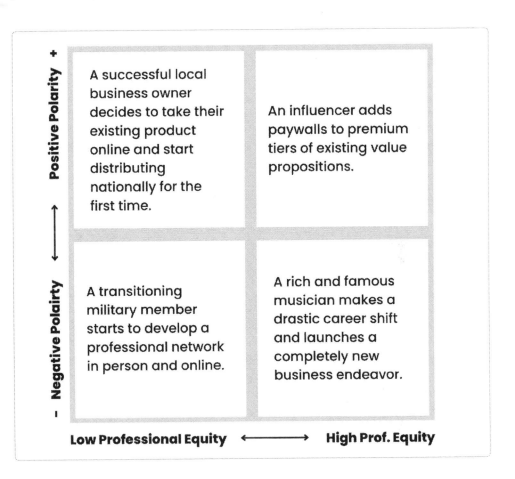

DIGGING DEEPER INTO NETWORK POLARITY

Separating this concept into four quadrants is a bit reductive as each axis is a wide, variable spectrum, and we all fall onto a different spot on the graph. A firm understanding of these quadrants, however, will inform your approach to the platform. The following are examples of where veterans in different positions or career phases sit on the graph. At the end of this section, you should be able to take all of the personas in the "don't be that guy/gal" section and place them into a quadrant rather easily.

Note: In the following section, I mention examples of veteran influencers on LinkedIn who fall into these categories to put them into a wider context, and these examples should not necessarily be interpreted as an endorsement of these folks, their content, or their business endeavors.

Negative Polarity / Low Professional Equity

- ✦ Examples: YOU right now, in all likelihood. Nearly every single military transitioner falls into this category, especially when on the hunt for employment and new to LinkedIn or professional network development.

- ✦ Advantages: gets to play the "new guy/new girl" card. Will be able to develop, lurk/observe, and learn almost entirely unseen.

- ✦ Disadvantages: patience is required. Acting like a "taker" here will come off as desperate and could thwart future networking attempts.

Positive Polarity / Low Professional Equity

- ✦ Examples: a veteran with quality insights and original ideas to share who already has a job and is not seeking anything at the time being. This will be you after you get that first gig.

- ✦ Advantages: low stakes. For now. This is the best time to develop consistent habits and slowly build your online network.

- ✦ Disadvantages: it can be easy to become complacent and put networking on the back burner when you're not currently in a state of need.

Negative Polarity / High Professional Equity

- ✦ Example: Veterati co-founder and CEO Daniel Rau and Redline Steel CEO Colin Wayne. Daniel is a well-known founder and has created a huge organization with a massive positive impact on the veteran community but doesn't post on LinkedIn often. Colin has a small LinkedIn network despite being in high demand for syndicated TV interviews and speaking gigs worldwide. If either were to dive headfirst into LinkedIn content creation just for the sake of developing that network and not for product sales, they would technically begin with a negative polarity.

- ✦ Advantages: can encourage followers and fans from other platforms to follow you on LinkedIn. Growth can be rapid.

- ✦ Disadvantages: many in this position diversify by expanding into new platforms without a real strategy or plan. If you're asking for new followers on a new platform, make sure you quickly give them a reason to follow you.

- ✸ Example: Chief Master Sergeant of the Air Force JoAnne Bass. JoAnne has developed a massive and engaged LinkedIn platform. Her content is insightful and inspiring and seeks only to provide value and celebrate others.

- ✸ Advantages: In this position, you can do a lot of good for a lot of people.

- ✸ Disadvantages: If someone in this position engages with their audience like a "taker," they will be condemned as a conman or grifter.

NETWORKING WITH A NEGATIVE POLARITY

Why does all of this matter? Well, most military members in the middle of career transitions have negative network polarities in almost every category. They're looking to grow a network—often for the first time—establish themselves as trusted voices in their industries, and are seeking employment. All negative polarities. To make matters worse, transitioners are often seeking post-service employment in an industry that they have little to no civilian work experience in. Again, this isn't necessarily a bad thing, but it definitely should inform your approach to whatever platform you're networking through.

I've seen many higher-ranking commissioned and non-commissioned officers struggle in transition after retirement due to a misinterpretation of their professional equity polarity. Simply put, they often believe they're destined for the C-Suite fresh out of the military. Though I've seen it happen a few times, that assumption is a mistake. More commonly, I've seen folks in this position approach their post-service job hunt as if they're God's gift to the civilian workforce in an over-inflated sense of positive polarity, only to have their expectations come crashing down around them.

Did these outstanding professionals have a ton to bring to the table for potential employers? Absolutely. But time and time again, transitioners fail to understand that they're in a position of need—of negative polarity—and fail to dedicate themselves accordingly to becoming students of their transition and post-service job hunt, which is necessary in most cases.

Giving and providing value to others should be your number one priority, especially if you're in a position of negative polarity and low equity. Ask questions, share resources and lessons learned, and be helpful. That's hands down the most effective way to convey your value and subject-matter expertise while expanding your network. LinkedIn, as it happens, is currently the best place for professionals to do all of the above.

CHAPTER 15

Being a Conduit

As we talked about, there's nothing more powerful when it comes to giving your equity a boost than connecting others. Being known as a "guy/gal who knows a guy/gal" is probably the biggest feather you can have in your equity cap. Have your radar up at all times for opportunities to connect with kindred spirits or help others solve problems through new relationships. When I see a fruitful interconnection opportunity, I usually send both parties direct messages informing them that I'll be introducing them to someone who I feel would be a valuable connection. Then I write a group message to them linking them up.

"Hi Jane and John—I wanted to connect you two awesome people. Jane, John is the owner of Johnny's Cookie Company and is looking for potential opportunities to donate his cookies to worthy charitable causes. John, Jane is the CEO of the Kids Need Cookies Foundation, a nonprofit dedicated to giving cookies to children in need. Seems like it could be a great fit! I'll let you two take it from here. Have a great week!"

If John and Jane are able to establish a mutually beneficial connection, they'll never forget that you were the one who selflessly took the time to make the introduction.

The last sentiment in the above paragraph is an important one. "I'll let you take it from here," is a polite way of saying, "If you two are going to talk, do it in your own DMs, because I sure don't need to have my messages and notifications clogged up with you exchanging niceties and coordinating a time to chat in a group message that no longer has anything to do with me." Trust me, you'll be glad you threw that part in.

Be careful, though. When you make a connection or referral like this, you are always accepting some degree of risk. Your reputation—and your equity—become vulnerable, so be sure to think it through. Don't be so eager to connect folks that you make a mistake. Remember, there are "givers" and "takers"' on LinkedIn. Never refer "takers" to your precious network connections. Unleashing snake oil salespeople upon your network can easily obliterate your professional equity.

Often, your connections will comb through your network—if it's visible to them—to find potentially advantageous connections, then request that you make the introduction. This is normal, but always be skeptical. Ask yourself:

- ✸ Do I know this person well?

- ✸ Do I trust this person?

- ✸ Do I trust that they're a 'giver' and not a 'taker?

This is where sales professionals and financial advisers have the biggest uphill challenge, as most LinkedIn users are highly skeptical of those professions. I never make referrals unless I'm 100% certain that the person won't be making a pitch.

Asking for a referral yourself doesn't necessarily make you a "taker" either, as long as you approach it the right way. If you're seeking a referral from a mutual connection in hopes of making a pitch or adding someone to a mailing list or a sales pipeline, think again. Doing so will put your connection in a very uncomfortable position, and you could do real damage to their professional equity. On the other hand, let's say you're nearing your military separation, plan to relocate to Boston, and hope to work in cyber security. If you wish to leverage an existing connection to get an introduction, here is how I suggest going about it.

✸ Create an original post explaining exactly that

Vets love to help other vets. You may be surprised by how many people rally around you. They may tag the very person you're looking for in reply to your post or reach out in a direct message offering to make a connection without you even asking. I've seen it happen a thousand times.

✸ Comb through the networks of your most trusted LinkedIn pals

Use your search features to taper down their connections. Are they connected with anyone in Boston? Are they connected with anyone who works in tech in Boston? Are they connected with anyone who works specifically in cyber security in Boston? What about veterans who work in cyber security in Boston? Jackpot. The more logical connection points, the better. The best foundational connection point is mutual service.

✸ Reach out to your connection and ask if they could kindly refer you to this person

You may not get a reply right away or at all, and that's okay. Don't harass your connection. Unfortunately, not everyone checks LinkedIn every day. Or they may be uncomfortable with your request and are ghosting you. Don't take it personally.

✸ And if you get the connection you're looking for . . .

And you might, even though you have a negative polarity because you're seeking employment in this arena. Remember to approach your conversation with a "giver" mentality. Ditch any sense of entitlement, cut to the chase, and don't ask for handout.

Try this:

"Hi Jane—it's a pleasure to be connected with you. Like Dave said, I'll be relocating to your neck of the woods once my service commitment is up. I'd be honored to have you in my LinkedIn network."

Then just leave it.

The last part of this breakdown can be the absolute hardest for people to understand. You haven't missed an opportunity by not shooting your shot at the first available moment. If you're doing this thing right, your new connection will see the content that you're posting frequently and see that you're engaging with their content as well as with their peers. If they have the capacity or desire to help, they'll often offer it up without you even asking.

You may be thinking—Wait just a minute. You don't want me to ask if she knows of any available positions? I shouldn't attach my résumé? What's the point? No, heck no, and the point is to develop your network in a positive and organic fashion. The higher your professional equity and the more network karma points you have saved up, the more powerful it will be when you finally express a need. And if you're being a "giver," hopefully people will want to help without you having to bring it up. Remember, you're planting seeds to harvest later.

Gary Vaynerchuk would say that you need to throw a bunch of jabs before the right hook. I came up with a more illustrative and entirely ridiculous analogy.

When I was a kid, Super Soakers were all the rage. These weren't just squirt guns. No sir. These were unregulated weapons of mass destruction. If you managed to prime the pump of these bad boys enough times—after a hundred or so pumps you had to put your entire body into it or get help from a friend—you could decimate the competition.

Some kids just pumped a few times and hopped into battle. Pump, pump, squirt. Pump, pump, squirt. Fools.

I was the kid who sat in the corner and pumped my Super Soaker until the ultra-thick plastic holding tank bowed out precariously. Once it was on the verge of explosion, I entered the fray. Few walked away to tell the tale. One blast could straight-up knock a toddler off his tiny feet.

Pump up your network by giving, serving, and building good professional karma. Do it beyond your comfort zone. While other folks are pumping a few times and shooting their shots with minimal returns, sit in the corner and patiently build up the pressure. When the time comes to shoot, the result will be explosive.

THE VETERAN FRATERNITY

It's wise to start expanding your network on LinkedIn—and elsewhere—by leveraging your extended veteran family first. We talked about how one of the most advantageous approaches to network development is through finding common threads, and there are few deep-rooted experiences more powerful than the shared experiences of the veteran community. Often, the veteran brother and sisterhood is powerful enough to overcome any sort of distance or disparity in your professional equity polarity. In other words, it's strong enough to neutralize network polarity. There are a couple of important considerations though.

⊛ **Veterans and veteran groups can be fickle and cliquey.**

Always engage with a positive attitude, especially as it pertains to other vets who may not be in the room or conversation at the time. If the clique finds you toxic, you can be excommunicated very quickly. I've seen it happen. If others are trashing people, stay above it. And remember, they could do the same to you in the next breath. Avoid folks like that.

⊛ **Leave any sense of entitlement or ego at the door, and again, don't be a "taker."**

Working veteran professionals and entrepreneurs, in my experience, are exceptionally impatient with veterans who act as if they're owed something by virtue of their service. Being an outspoken, entitlement brat can make our whole community look bad.

⊛ **While it behooves you to engage with your veteran brothers and sisters, make sure you branch out in equal measure.**

If you network exclusively with veterans and never venture from that bubble, it can stunt your civilian business and career progression and hinder your ability to fully transition back into the civilian world. Though I can sympathize with the temptation to stick with your military ilk where it's comfortable, I can't recommend highly enough against doing so. Unfortunately, I've seen that happen countless times. And it hasn't been good.

PERSONALITY AND STORYTELLING

As your personal brand, post-service career, and network matures, you may notice some subtle changes in yourself and how your network reacts and interacts with you. You'll be asking, needing, and seeking less. But at the same time, more people will be reaching out to you in need. You may get more notifications, clout-chaser tags, or job offers than you know what to do with. You may land your dream job. You may be asked to share your thoughts in a blog, live stream, or podcast. The opportunities are endless and exciting. You may even experience your first real cross-platform trolling, which is not as thrilling.

You might start to feel more comfortable and allow your personality to shine through. Ideally, be yourself from the onset, but I can sympathize with the apprehension many feel to do so on LinkedIn. I definitely kept things as professional as possible when I was getting started, but over time, I found my voice and allowed my goofier side to come through. This process may be accelerated if you discover a passion for content creation and storytelling. Far from the public perception of mindless, inflexible robots, military members are commonly quite adept at storytelling.

It's an exceptional avenue of self-expression for veterans. It can help us heal, overcome adversity, and approach challenging circumstances with balance, perspective, and confidence. Many of us aren't sure where to start or how to share our stories, which can be frustrating for those veterans who are bursting with things to say.

HEADS UP!

LinkedIn frequently sends out emails requesting user feedback in a brief survey. Occasionally, they will compensate you for your time with a small gift card. If you become a reliable enough contributor or fit a specific demographic they are seeking information from, they may invite you to do a remote, one-on-one feedback session with a LinkedIn representative.

Not only is this an awesome way to help shape the course of the platform, but these sessions may net you over $100.

Be aware, always, of scams and phishing attempts in your inbox. Always question and verify the sources of any emails you may receive, and be cautious about clicking links from unknown sources.

I'm often asked about posting content in the "right way." New creators take the time to put pen to paper and don't want their efforts to go to waste, which is commendable. They agonize over how to post, where to post, and when to post. Sometimes anxiety dissuades folks from posting in the first place and makes the idea of sharing content frequently seem daunting and exhausting. For everyone who feels that way, fret not. You've got it all wrong.

If it were true that your carefully written story only had one opportunity to be presented to the world, well, no author or content creator would be able to stay consistent. The workload would be ridiculous. In reality, you can get a ton of mileage out of one story across multiple platforms, whether it's one paragraph or ten pages long. Your story can—and should—wear a lot of different hats. Let's say you write a 2,500-word blog article. Here are all the things you could do with that content.

⊛ Publish the article through LinkedIn's native publisher (1). Share the link on Facebook (2), on Twitter (3), and in a private LinkedIn group inviting your pals to read and share it (4).

⊛ Publish the article on Medium (5) or your own website (6). Make a LinkedIn post inviting people to go read your new article on Medium (7).

⊛ Reach out to local publications—digital or traditional—inviting them to cross-post your article (8). If you get published in your local paper, share a post about it on Facebook (9), LinkedIn (10), and Twitter (11). Put a picture of the article in print on Instagram (12).

⊛ Find a favorite quote or short passage, and post it on Facebook (13), LinkedIn (14), Twitter (15), or anywhere else you're active, inviting your network to read and share their feedback. Include the link to the article. Now do that for another quote (16, 17, 18). And another (19, 20, 21). And another (22, 23, 24). You should be able to find at least three quote-worthy phrases in a 2500-word article!

⊛ And as a bonus, read your favorite quotes from above in a short candid video, and share on TikTok (25), YouTube shorts (26), or Instagram Reels (27).

From a single article, I was able to quickly brainstorm at least twenty-four ways to share the article and content ripped from the article. That's two posts per month for a whole year, all from one piece of content. If anyone replies in a substantive or thoughtful way, you can screen cap it and make a new post about it. If a troll unleashes on you, you can make a post about that too. Get as much mileage as possible. Take your content oranges and squeeze every last little drop of goodness out of them. You can even repeat the cycle.

It would be impossible to maintain producing a fresh piece of content every single day. It would also be downright tragic if the fruit of your labor was only allowed to live for one fleeting instant. But take heart. Literally nobody does that. Not even the biggest and most active influencers. They allow their content to wear different hats and often reuse their best pieces. You may be asking, "But doesn't that mean I'm being unoriginal? Will I have to worry about people calling me out for recycling old stuff?"

Nope. Seriously, don't sweat it. And if creating all of those pieces of content seems like a big lift, please bear in mind that I never said you had to do it all at once. It's a lot easier than writing an original article every day at least, isn't it?

In Conclusion

I despise long, drawn out conclusions, so I'll make mine snappy.

Whatever your personal goals are and however your professional journey unfolds, your overall approach must remain consistent if you wish to reap long-term benefits from your LinkedIn network. Those long-term benefits are shared by you and other LinkedIn users who could be inspired by your contributions. You may be more selective about how you allocate your time and efforts if your circumstances change, but never lose focus on showing up, participating, giving, and helping. This isn't just about establishing good karmic vibes!

What happens if you find yourself in need down the road, holding a negative polarity in a new arena? What if you gave up on LinkedIn the second you landed a gig, then got laid off? If I had a dollar for every veteran I've witnessed abandon LinkedIn once they got a job, I'd be able to afford a $12,000 life coach. It's sad to see, and it's also extremely shortsighted.

It's a lot like training for a marathon. You can't exactly cram for the big day. Besides, if you devote yourself to being a connector, sharer, inspirer, and contributor only to disappear after landing a gig, then you were never truly committed to being a "giver," were you?

As your influence grows, you may become a trusted voice in an industry, discipline, or demographic. Please take this responsibility seriously. Never stop being kind, and never stop giving, especially to your veteran brothers and sisters. Remember how it felt when you were on the heels of your transition. Think about how many amazing people bent over backward to provide you with the support you needed to succeed after service. Pay it forward. Everyone's journey is different, and each service member walking out their path deserves to be treated with respect and dignity.

If you found this guide to be helpful and feel like others would benefit from it, please take a moment to review it on Amazon or wherever you purchased it. It helps a lot! Additionally, I'm committed to providing ongoing support. Please don't hesitate to reach out to me on LinkedIn and join my exclusive network development community. There's no catch. I merely want to do everything that I can to ensure that veterans and military families have the resources they need to thrive after service.

I am committed to providing you with evergreen support. Click the link or scan the QR code to join my exclusive online community.

🌐 *https://community.adambraatz.com*

Rooting for your holistic fulfillment,

Adam Braatz

Made in the USA
Columbia, SC
17 October 2022

69538594R10076